Better Homes & Gardens.

CHRISTMAS COOKING
FROM THE HEART™

Festive Season

Meredith Consumer Marketing
Des Moines, Iowa

CHRISTMAS COOKING
FROM THE HEART™

MEREDITH CORPORATION CONSUMER MARKETING
Consumer Marketing Product Director: Daniel Fagan
Consumer Marketing Product Manager: Max Daily
Consumer Products Marketing Manager: Kylie Dazzo
Business Manager: Diane Umland
Senior Production Manager: Al Rodruck

WATERBURY PUBLICATIONS, INC.
Editorial Director: Lisa Kingsley
Creative Director: Ken Carlson
Associate Editor: Tricia Bergman
Associate Design Director: Doug Samuelson
Production Assistant: Mindy Samuelson
Contributing Copy Editor: Peg Smith
Contributing Proofreader: Terri Fredrickson
Contributing Food Stylist: Jennifer Peterson

BETTER HOMES & GARDENS *MAGAZINE*
Editor in Chief: Stephen Orr
Creative Director: Jennifer D. Madara
Executive Editor: Oma Blaise Ford

MEREDITH CORPORATION
President and CEO: Tom Harty
Executive Chairman: Stephen M. Lacy

In Memoriam: E.T. Meredith III (1933–2003)

Better Homes & Gardens.
TEST KITCHEN

Our seal assures you that every recipe in *Christmas Cooking from the Heart*™ has been tested in the *Better Homes & Gardens* Test Kitchen. This means that each recipe is practical and reliable and it meets our high standards of taste appeal. We guarantee your satisfaction with this book for as long as you own it.

All of us at Meredith Consumer Marketing are dedicated to providing you with information and ideas to enhance your home. We welcome your comments and suggestions. Write to us at: Meredith Consumer Marketing, 1716 Locust St, Des Moines, IA 50309-3023. *Christmas Cooking from the Heart*™ is available by mail. To order editions from past years, call 800/627-5490.

Cover: Coconut Layer Cake
(recipe, page 82)

SUGAR COOKIES,
PAGE 98

COFFEE SHAKE SHOTS,
PAGE 37

Table of Contents

Festive Season

This festive time of year brings busy days with gatherings both large and small. Whether you're hosting an annual cookie exchange, cooking for formal family dinner, or entertaining friends for the New Year, you need delicious recipes that you can count on. That's what *Better Homes & Gardens® Christmas Cooking from the Heart*™ is all about—recipes and ideas tailored to holiday gatherings. For a sparkling holiday party to kick off the season, choose from small bites with big flavor: Prosciutto-Wrapped Scallops with Roasted Red Pepper Aïoli (page 29), Pimiento Cheese Pull-Apart Christmas Tree (page 34), and festive Party Punch (page 38). Gather family around the table for a feast featuring Porketta Roast (page 10), Cheesy Baked Gnocchi with Kale (page 16), and Citrus Couscous Salad (page 20). Fill cookie platters and gift boxes with Lady Baltimore Tassies (page 98), Cherry-Almond Half Moons (page 105), and Salted Caramel Brownies with Pretzel Crust (page 110). Ring in the New Year with nibbles both savory and sweet—Bacon-Almond Potato Croquettes (page 137), Flatbread with Balsamic Greens and Prosciutto (page 133), and S'mores Cheesecake (page 142). Happy Cooking and Happy Holidays!

PIMIENTO CHEESE
PULL-APART
CHRISTMAS TREE,
PAGE 34

MUSHROOM BISQUE
WITH LEMON
GREMOLATA, PAGE 24

Celebration Dinners

Discover inspiring and impressive recipes here to make memorable main dishes, salads, sides, and soups for family and friends.

ORANGE-ROASTED
CHICKEN, PAGE 12

9

2. Grill roast over indirect heat, covered, 1½ to 2¼ hours or until an instant-read thermometer registers 150°F. Transfer meat to a warm platter. Cover and let stand 15 minutes before carving. Makes 9 servings.

PER SERVING *225 cal., 11 g fat (4 g sat. fat), 87 mg chol., 129 mg sodium, 0 g carb., 0 g fiber, 29 g pro.*

RED WINE POT ROAST

PREP 30 minutes
SLOW COOK 10 hours (low) or 5 hours (high)

2 Tbsp. olive oil
1 2- to 2½-lb. boneless beef chuck pot roast, trimmed
2 cloves garlic, minced
¾ cup dry red wine
1 lb. tiny new red potatoes
4 large carrots, cut into 1½-inch pieces
2 cups 1-inch pieces peeled rutabaga
1 cup 1-inch pieces celery
2 Tbsp. tomato paste
¾ cup reduced-sodium beef broth
2 Tbsp. quick-cooking tapioca, crushed
1 tsp. dried thyme, crushed
½ tsp. salt
½ tsp. black pepper

1. In a large skillet heat oil over medium-high heat. Add meat; cook until browned on both sides. Transfer meat to a 6-quart slow cooker. Add garlic to hot skillet; cook and stir 1 minute. Add wine to pan, stirring to scrape up any brown bits. Pour wine, garlic, and remaining ingredients (through pepper) over meat in slow cooker.

2. Cover and cook on low 10 to 11 hours or high 5 to 5½ hours. Using a slotted spoon, transfer meat and vegetables to a platter. Skim fat from cooking liquid. Season to taste with additional salt and pepper. Serve meat and vegetables with cooking liquid. Makes 6 servings.

PER SERVING *382 cal., 11 g fat (3 g sat. fat), 98 mg chol., 471 mg sodium, 27 g carb., 5 g fiber, 37 g pro.*

PORKETTA ROAST

PORKETTA ROAST

PREP 20 minutes
GRILL 1 hour 30 minutes
STAND 15 minutes

2 Tbsp. snipped fresh parsley
1 tsp. fennel seeds, crushed
1 tsp. minced dried onion
½ tsp. dried rosemary, crushed
½ tsp. dried oregano, crushed
¼ tsp. salt
¼ tsp. garlic powder
¼ tsp. ground cloves
⅛ tsp. ground coriander
1 3- to 4-lb. boneless pork top loin roast, (double loin, tied)

1. In a small bowl stir together the first nine ingredients (through coriander). Rub all over roast.

RED WINE
POT ROAST

ORANGE-ROASTED CHICKEN

PREP 20 minutes
ROAST 20 minutes at 450°F plus 1 hour at 350°F
STAND 10 minutes

7   clementines or desired oranges
1   3½- to 4-lb. whole chicken
1   tsp. kosher salt
½   tsp. freshly cracked black pepper
4   strips bacon
12 fresh sage leaves
⅓   cup pure maple syrup
¼   cup dry sherry
1   Tbsp. extra-virgin olive oil
3   cloves garlic, minced

1. Preheat oven to 450°F. Halve all seven clementines. Thinly slice four halves into half-moons; set aside.

2. Rinse chicken body cavity; pat dry. Season inside and outside of chicken with salt and black pepper. Place one clementine half in cavity. Twist wing tips under back; tie drumsticks together using 100-percent-cotton kitchen string. Place breast side up in a 13×9-inch baking pan or dish.
3. Lay bacon lengthwise on chicken breast; tuck six sage leaves and all clementine slices under bacon.
4. For vinaigrette, over a small bowl juice four clementine halves. Whisk in maple syrup, sherry, oil, and garlic; set aside.
5. Place remaining five clementine halves around chicken. Chop remaining sage leaves; sprinkle over clementines. Roast chicken 20 minutes. Spoon half the vinaigrette over chicken. Reduce heat to 350°F; cover chicken with foil.

Roast 50 to 60 minutes, spooning remaining vinaigrette over chicken every 15 minutes. Remove and set aside foil.
6. Roast 10 minutes more or until a thermometer inserted into thigh registers 170°F. Cover with foil; let stand 10 minutes. To serve, squeeze one roasted clementine half over chicken. Makes 4 servings.
PER SERVING *603 cal., 19 g fat (6 g sat. fat), 204 mg chol., 882 mg sodium, 33 g carb., 2 g fiber, 64 g pro.*

BACON-BLUE CHEESE MASHED POTATOES

PREP 30 minutes
COOK 20 minutes

3   lb. russet, Yukon gold, or red potatoes, peeled (if desired) and cut into 2-inch pieces
¼   cup butter
½   to ¾ cup milk, heavy cream, or half-and-half
6   slices bacon, chopped
1½   cups crumbled blue cheese (6 oz.)
1   tsp. salt
½   tsp. black pepper
¼   cup thinly sliced green onions
     Melted butter (optional)

1. In a covered 4- to 5-quart Dutch oven cook potatoes in enough lightly salted boiling water to cover 20 to 25 minutes or until tender; drain. Return potatoes to hot Dutch oven. Add ¼ cup butter; let stand, uncovered, 2 to 3 minutes.
2. Meanwhile, in a small saucepan heat milk over low heat until hot but not boiling. In a medium skillet cook bacon over medium heat until crisp. Drain on paper towels.
3. Mash potatoes just until light and fluffy. Stir in warm milk, cheese, salt, and pepper. If needed, stir in additional milk to reach desired consistency. Sprinkle with bacon and green onions. If desired, drizzle with melted butter. Makes 10 servings.
PER SERVING *238 cal., 12 g fat (7 g sat. fat), 31 mg chol., 557 mg sodium, 26 g carb., 2 g fiber, 9 g pro.*

ORANGE-ROASTED
CHICKEN

BACON-BLUE CHEESE
MASHED POTATOES

CARAWAY
WHOLE-ROASTED
CAULIFLOWER

CARAWAY WHOLE-ROASTED CAULIFLOWER

PREP 30 minutes
BAKE 30 minutes at 425°F plus 30 minutes at 450°F

2   Tbsp. extra-virgin olive oil
1   Tbsp. stone-ground mustard
2   tsp. caraway seeds, toasted and crushed
1   tsp. kosher salt
1   2- to 2½-lb. head cauliflower, trimmed
¼   cup water
½   cup sliced red onion
⅓   cup red wine vinegar
1   tsp. sugar
½   tsp. kosher salt
¼   cup snipped dried apricots
    Stone-ground mustard (optional)
    Rye bread (optional)

1. Preheat oven to 425°F. In a small bowl whisk together olive oil, mustard, caraway seeds, and salt. Spread mustard mixture on the cauliflower. Place water into an 8- to 10-inch cast iron or other oven-going skillet. Place cauliflower in skillet; cover with foil.
2. Bake 30 minutes. Meanwhile, for pickled onions, in a small bowl combine onion, vinegar, sugar, and salt; set aside, stirring occasionally.
3. Uncover cauliflower. Increase oven temperature to 450°F. Continue roasting, uncovered, 30 minutes, or until golden brown and tender. Serve with pickled onions, dried apricots, and, if desired, mustard and rye bread. Makes 4 servings.
PER SERVING *115 cal., 7 g fat (1 g sat. fat), 0 mg chol., 390 mg sodium, 12 g carb., 3 g fiber, 2 g pro.*

ROASTED CARROTS AND ORANGES

PREP 20 minutes
BAKE 40 minutes at 425°F

5   navel or other oranges
2   lb. multicolor or orange carrots with 1- to 2-inch tops, peeled and halved if large
3   Tbsp. extra-virgin olive oil
1   tsp. kosher salt
5   pitted dates
¼   cup water
1   Tbsp. apple cider vinegar
½   tsp. paprika

ROASTED CARROTS AND ORANGES

½   tsp. ground chipotle chile pepper
½   tsp. freshly cracked black pepper

1. Preheat oven to 425°F. Thinly slice two and one-half oranges; set aside. Zest one orange; set zest aside. Juice zested orange and remaining one and a half oranges (for about ⅔ cup juice. Set aside ⅓ cup for dressing. Use remaining juice in Step 2).
2. Line a large roasting pan with foil. In a large bowl combine orange slices and ⅓ cup juice, the carrots, 1 tablespoon oil, and ½ teaspoon salt; toss to coat. Transfer to pan. Roast 20 minutes. Gently turn carrots and oranges. Roast 20 minutes more or just until carrots are tender and lightly browned.
3. Meanwhile, for dressing, in a small food processor or blender combine dates and water. Cover; pulse until nearly smooth. Add orange zest and reserved ⅓ cup juice, remaining 2 tablespoons oil, the vinegar, paprika, chipotle chile pepper, remaining salt, and black pepper; set aside. Cover; process to combine. Drizzle carrots and oranges with half the dressing; pass remaining. Makes 4 servings.
PER SERVING *258 cal., 11 g fat (2 g sat. fat), 0 mg chol., 571 mg sodium, 41 g carb., 9 g fiber, 3 g pro.*

BACON-ROASTED
SWEET POTATOES AND
SHALLOTS WITH
BLISTERED GRAPES

**CHEESY
BAKED
GNOCCHI
WITH KALE**

CHEESY BAKED GNOCCHI WITH KALE

PREP 20 minutes
BAKE 20 minutes at 400°F

2   16-oz. pkg. gnocchi
1   bunch kale, washed, stemmed, and chopped
3   cloves garlic, minced
2   Tbsp. butter
2   Tbsp. all-purpose flour
1½ cups milk
½   cup shredded Fontina or sharp white cheddar cheese
1   Tbsp. lemon zest
½   cup finely shredded Parmesan cheese

1. Preheat oven to 400°F. Grease a 2-quart baking dish; set aside. In a large pot cook gnocchi according to package directions, adding kale the last 1 minute. Drain; return pasta and kale to pot.
2. Meanwhile, in a saucepan cook garlic in butter over medium heat 1 minute. Stir in flour to combine. Whisk in milk; cook and stir until thickened and bubbly. Stir in Fontina and lemon zest. Pour over gnocchi mixture; stir to coat. Transfer to prepared baking dish. Top with Parmesan. Bake 20 minutes, until lightly browned and bubbly. Makes 6 servings.
PER SERVING *444 cal., 11 g fat (6 g sat. fat), 31 mg chol., 749 mg sodium, 71 g carb., 4 g fiber, 18 g pro.*

BACON-ROASTED SWEET POTATOES AND SHALLOTS WITH BLISTERED GRAPES

PREP 25 minutes
ROAST 30 minutes at 450°F

8   oz. bacon, coarsely chopped
2¼ lb. sweet potatoes, cut into 2-inch pieces
10 oz. shallots, peeled and halved or quartered
½   tsp. kosher salt
½   tsp. pepper
2   cups red or green seedless grapes

1. Preheat oven to 450°F. In a large skillet cook bacon until crisp. Reserve 3 tablespoons drippings in skillet/pan and drain bacon on paper towels. Place a 15×10-inch baking pan in oven 5 minutes.
2. In a large bowl toss together the sweet potatoes, bacon drippings, shallots, salt, and pepper. Transfer to hot baking pan. Roast 30 minutes or until tender, stirring once and adding grapes the last 5 minutes of roasting. Top with bacon. Makes 8 servings.
PER SERVING *260 cal., 9 g fat (3 g sat. fat), 16 mg chol., 352 mg sodium, 39 g carb., 5 g fiber, 7 g pro.*

BALSAMIC ROASTED
BRUSSELS SPROUTS
WITH BACON

BALSAMIC ROASTED BRUSSELS SPROUTS WITH BACON

PREP 15 minutes
ROAST 15 minutes at 400°F

2   lb. Brussels sprouts, trimmed and halved or quartered
¼   cup balsamic vinegar
2   Tbsp. olive oil
½   tsp. salt
½   tsp. black pepper
4   slices bacon, crisp-cooked, drained, and crumbled
1   Tbsp. lemon zest (optional)

1. Preheat oven to 400°F. Line a large baking pan with foil. Place Brussels sprouts in prepared pan. Drizzle with half the vinegar and the oil; sprinkle with salt and pepper; toss to coat.

2. Roast 15 to 20 minutes or until sprouts are crisp-tender and browned, stirring frequently.

3. Drizzle with remaining vinegar, sprinkle with bacon and, if desired, lemon zest. Makes 8 servings.

PER SERVING *104 cal., 5 g fat (1 g sat. fat), 4 mg chol., 242 mg sodium, 12 g carb., 4 g fiber, 5 g pro.*

GRUYÈRE RISOTTO WITH
ARUGULA GREMOLATA

GRUYÈRE RISOTTO WITH ARUGULA GREMOLATA

PREP 25 minutes
SLOW COOK 1 hour 15 minutes (high)
STAND 15 minutes

⅔ cup sliced leeks
2 cloves garlic, minced
1 Tbsp. butter
1¾ cups uncooked arborio rice
4 cups reduced-sodium chicken broth
⅔ cup dry white wine
½ tsp. cracked black pepper
2 oz. Gruyère or Swiss cheese, shredded (½ cup)
1 recipe Arugula Gremolata

1. In a large skillet cook leeks and garlic in hot butter over medium heat 3 to 5 minutes or until tender. Stir in rice; cook and stir 1 minute more. Spoon into a 3½- or 4-quart slow cooker. Stir in broth, wine, and pepper.

2. Cover and cook on high 1¼ hours or until rice is tender. Remove crockery liner from cooker, if possible, or turn off cooker. Let risotto stand, uncovered, 15 minutes before serving. Top with cheese and Arugula Gremolata. Makes 4 servings.

Arugula Gremolata In a small bowl stir together 1 cup snipped fresh arugula; 1-oz. prosciutto, crisp-cooked, drained, and crumbled; 2 tablespoons chopped toasted pine nuts; 1 tablespoon lemon zest; and 1 clove garlic, minced.

PER SERVING *510 cal., 13 g fat (5 g sat. fat), 26 mg chol., 828 mg sodium, 74 g carb., 3 g fiber, 20 g pro.*

KALE, CRANBERRY, AND ROOT VEGETABLE SALAD

PREP 30 minutes
ROAST 30 minutes at 425°F
STAND 30 minutes

3 medium beets, trimmed, peeled, quartered ,and cut in ¼-inch slices
5 medium carrots, cut in ¼-inch slices
3 Tbsp. olive oil
½ tsp. sea salt
½ tsp. cracked black pepper
4 medium shallots, quartered lengthwise

KALE, CRANBERRY, AND ROOT VEGETABLE SALAD

¾ cup fresh or frozen cranberries, coarsely chopped
1 8-oz. bunch kale, stems removed and leaves cut into ½-inch wide ribbons
⅓ cup golden raisins
2 Tbsp. lemon juice
1 Tbsp. honey mustard
2 cloves garlic, minced
1 tsp. grated fresh ginger
¼ cup chopped pecans, toasted (tip, page 34)

1. Place a large rimmed baking sheet in oven; preheat oven to 425°F. Meanwhile, in an extra-large bowl combine beets, carrots, 2 tablespoons oil, salt, and pepper. Carefully add beets and carrots to hot pan in a single layer; set bowl aside. Roast 10 minutes. Add shallots and cranberries to pan, stirring to coat. Roast 20 to 25 minutes or just until vegetables are tender, stirring once.

2. Meanwhile, place kale in a bowl. Add remaining 1 tablespoon oil. Massage kale with your hands 2 to 4 minutes, or until bright green and tender. In a small bowl combine raisins, lemon juice, mustard, garlic, and ginger.

3. When vegetables are tender, remove pan from oven; add raisin mixture and stir to coat. Cool 5 minutes. Add all to kale; toss to coat. Let stand 30 minutes. To serve, top with pecans. Makes 10 servings.

PER SERVING *154 cal., 7 g fat (1 g sat. fat), 0 mg chol., 156 mg sodium, 20 g carb., 5 g fiber, 5 g pro.*

**CITRUS
COUSCOUS
SALAD**

to catch juices, cut each segment from membranes. (Or slice into wheels.)

4. For citrus oil, chop enough remaining orange zest strips to equal 1 tablespoon. In a large skillet combine chopped zest, remaining 3 tablespoons olive oil, the garlic, and thyme. Heat over low heat 5 minutes or until warm; set aside.

5. To serve, on a platter combine orange segments and juices, couscous, red onion, hazelnuts, and olives. Drizzle with red wine vinegar. Spoon citrus oil on salad. Sprinkle with salt and black pepper, and, if desired, crushed red pepper. Makes 6 servings.

PER SERVING *308 cal., 14 g fat (2 g sat. fat), 0 mg chol., 306 mg sodium, 41 g carb., 4 g fiber, 7 g pro.*

APPLE-BEET SALAD

START TO FINISH 40 minutes

1   lb. red beets, peeled and cut into thin wedges
1   5- to 8-oz. pkg. mesclun or spring mix
1   medium Fuji or Pink Lady apple, cored and cut into thin wedges
1   oz. goat cheese (chèvre), crumbled
2   Tbsp. chopped walnuts, toasted (tip, page 34)
2   Tbsp. cider vinegar
1   Tbsp. olive oil
1   tsp. finely chopped chives or green onion
½   tsp. Dijon mustard
¼   tsp. black pepper
⅛   tsp. salt

1. Cook beets, covered, in enough boiling salted water to cover, 20 minutes or until tender; drain.

2. Arrange mesclun on a serving platter. Top with beets, apple, goat cheese, and walnuts.

3. In a screw-top jar combine vinegar, olive oil, chives, mustard, pepper, and salt. Cover and shake well to combine. Drizzle over salad. Makes 6 servings.

PER SERVING *92 cal., 5 g fat (1 g sat. fat), 2 mg chol., 120 mg sodium, 10 g carb., 3 g fiber, 3 g pro.*

CITRUS COUSCOUS SALAD

PREP 30 minutes
COOK 20 minutes

6   large Cara Cara or navel oranges
4   Tbsp. extra-virgin olive oil
1   cup Israeli couscous
1¼   cups reduced-sodium chicken broth or vegetable broth
¼   tsp. coarse salt
3   cloves garlic, minced
1   Tbsp. chopped fresh thyme
1   cup very thinly sliced red onion
¼   cup blanched hazelnuts, toasted and coarsely chopped (tip, page 34)
¼   cup coarsely chopped, pitted Castelvetrano or Manzanilla olives
2   Tbsp. red wine vinegar

⅛   tsp. freshly cracked black pepper
    Crushed red pepper (optional)

1. Using a vegetable peeler remove strips of zest from one orange, avoiding white pith; set aside.

2. In a medium saucepan heat 1 tablespoon oil over medium heat. Add couscous; cook 2 minutes or until lightly toasted, stirring often. Add two orange zest strips, broth, and ¼ teaspoon salt. Bring to boiling over medium-high heat; reduce heat. Cover; cook 12 to 15 minutes or until couscous is tender and all liquid is absorbed. Cool; discard zest strips.

3. Meanwhile, using a paring knife, remove peel and pith from remaining oranges. Working over a small bowl

APPLE-BEET
SALAD

WALNUT-GRUYÈRE SCONES

PREP 20 minutes
BAKE 7 minutes at 350°F plus 18 minutes at 375°F

1¼   cups walnuts
2¼   cups all-purpose flour
2   tsp. baking powder
½   tsp. baking soda
¼   tsp. salt
½   cup cold butter
4   oz. Gruyère cheese, shredded
½   tsp. dried thyme, crushed, or
      1½ tsp. snipped fresh thyme
1   egg, lightly beaten
1   cup buttermilk
1   Tbsp. honey
1   Tbsp. Dijon mustard

1. Preheat oven to 350°F. Place walnuts on a large baking pan. Bake 7 to 9 minutes or until toasted. Coarsely chop 1 cup walnuts and finely grind remaining ¼ cup; set aside. Increase oven temperature to 375°F.
2. In a large bowl combine flour, ground walnuts, baking powder, baking soda, and salt. Using a pastry blender, cut in butter until mixture resembles coarse meal. Stir in Gruyère, the coarsely chopped walnuts, and thyme. Make a well in center of flour mixture. In a bowl combine egg, buttermilk, honey, and mustard; add all at once to flour mixture. Using a fork, stir just until moistened.
3. Turn dough out onto a lightly floured surface. Knead by folding and gently pressing 10 to 12 strokes or until nearly smooth. Divide in half. Pat or lightly roll each half to a ¾-inch-thick circle, about 6 inches in diameter. Cut each circle in eight triangles. Place triangles 2 inches apart on a greased baking sheet. Bake 18 to 20 minutes or until golden brown.
4. Transfer to cooling rack. If desired, top with additional cheese, walnuts, and thyme. Serve warm. Makes 16 servings.
PER SERVING *220 cal., 15 g fat (6 g sat. fat), 37 mg chol., 229 mg sodium, 17 g carb., 1 g fiber, 6 g pro.*

WALNUT-GRUYÈRE
SCONES

SESAME SEED-HERB PULL-APART WREATH

PREP 40 minutes
STAND 5 minutes
RISE 1 hour 30 minutes
REST 10 minutes
BAKE 15 minutes at 375°F

1   cup whole milk
⅓   cup sugar
2   pkg. active dry yeast (4½ tsp.)
¼   cup unsalted butter, softened
1½ tsp. salt
3   eggs
3¾ cups all-purpose flour
2   Tbsp. white sesame seeds
1   Tbsp. black sesame seeds
2   Tbsp. chopped fresh herbs or whole
    herb sprigs, such as oregano,
    thyme, rosemary, and/or sage

1. In a small saucepan heat the milk and sugar over medium heat just until warm (105°F to 115°F). Pour into a large bowl. Stir in yeast and let stand 5 minutes or until foamy. Add the butter, salt, two eggs, and 1 cup flour to milk mixture. Beat with a mixer on low until smooth. Stir in as much remaining flour as you can.
3. Transfer dough to a lightly floured surface. Knead in enough remaining flour to make a dough that is soft and smooth, but still a little sticky (about 4 minutes).
4. Butter a large bowl. Place dough in bowl, turning once to grease surface. Cover and let stand until double in size (about 1 hour).
5. Line a large baking sheet with parchment paper. Use a 12-inch plate as guide to draw a circle on the paper. Turn paper over.
6. Punch dough down. Turn out onto the floured surface. Cover; let rest 10 minutes. Divide dough into six even pieces. Pinch off six pieces from each dough piece, shaping each into a ball (36 total balls). Arrange 20 balls ½ inch apart on the paper circle. Arrange 16 balls about 1 inch inside the ring of dough balls (balls will touch). Cover loosely with a towel; let stand until dough is nearly doubled in size (about 30 minutes).
7. Preheat oven to 375°F. Beat the remaining egg with 1 tablespoon water. Gently brush tops of dough wreath with egg mixture. Sprinkle tops of wreath with seeds and herbs, or arrange whole herbs on top. Brush whole herbs with egg mixture. Bake 15 to 18 minutes or

ANDOUILLE CORN BREAD DRESSING

until golden brown. Serve warm or at room temperature. Makes 18 servings.
Make Ahead Bake and cool wreath as directed. Wrap in heavy foil. Freeze up to 1 month. To reheat, place frozen wrapped wreath in a 350°F oven 15 minutes or until warm.
PER SERVING *82 cal., 2 g fat (1 g sat. fat), 20 mg chol., 107 mg sodium, 13 g carb., 1 g fiber, 2 g pro.*

ANDOUILLE CORN BREAD DRESSING

PREP 30 minutes
SLOW COOK 3½ hours (low)

    Nonstick cooking spray
1   cup coarsely chopped onion
¾   cup coarsely chopped red sweet
    pepper
½   cup thinly sliced celery
⅓   cup butter
3   Tbsp. roasted, salted pepitas
2   Tbsp. snipped fresh sage or 2 tsp.
    dried sage, crushed
5   cups dried 1-inch cubes corn bread*
5   cups dried 1-inch cubes Texas toast*
1   13.5-oz. pkg. cooked, smoked
    andouille or chorizo sausage links,
    halved lengthwise and sliced
1   14.5-oz. can reduced-sodium
    chicken broth

1. Lightly coat a 3½- or 4-quart slow cooker with cooking spray. In a large skillet cook onion, sweet pepper, and celery in melted butter; cook 5 minutes or until softened, stirring occasionally. Stir in pumpkin seeds. Cook 3 minutes more or until vegetables are tender. Stir in sage.
2. In an extra-large bowl combine cubed corn bread and Texas toast, sausage, and vegetable mixture. Drizzle with broth to moisten, tossing lightly to combine. Transfer dressing to prepared cooker.
3. Cover and cook on low 3½ to 4 hours or until heated through. Makes 14 servings.
*Tip To dry bread cubes, preheat oven to 300°F. Cut corn bread and Texas toast into 1-inch cubes. Spread on two 15×10-inch baking pans. Bake 10 to 15 minutes or until dry, stirring twice; cool. (Bread will continue to dry and crisp as it cools.) Or let bread cubes stand, loosely covered, at room temperature 8 to 12 hours.
PER SERVING *272 cal., 16 g fat (6 g sat. fat), 42 mg chol., 600 mg sodium, 25 g carb., 2 g fiber, 8 g pro.*

3. If using low heat, turn to high. Stir together flour and butter; whisk into soup. Cover and cook 30 to 45 minutes more or until thickened and bubbly. Whisk in crème fraîche.

4. Meanwhile, for lemon gremolata, combine dill and lemon zest. Sprinkle servings with gremolata. Makes 8 servings.

PER SERVING *212 cal., 18 g fat (9 g sat. fat), 48 mg chol., 351 mg sodium, 9 g carb., 2 g fiber, 3 g pro.*

CORN-LENTIL CHOWDER

PREP 20 minutes
COOK 55 minutes

2   Tbsp. olive oil
1½ cups finely chopped yellow onion
1   Tbsp. curry powder
½   tsp. ground turmeric
1   32-oz. carton reduced-sodium chicken broth
2   cups water
1   Tbsp. peeled and grated fresh ginger
1½ cups dry yellow lentils, rinsed
1½ tsp. kosher salt
¼   tsp. black pepper
3   cups frozen corn
1   Tbsp. chili or olive oil
    Sour cream (optional)

1. In a large pot heat oil over medium-low heat. Add onion; cook 3 minutes or just until tender. Add curry powder and turmeric; cook 1 minute. Add broth, water, and ginger. Bring to boiling; reduce heat. Simmer, covered, 20 minutes.

2. Stir in lentils. Bring to boiling; reduce heat. Simmer, covered, 15 minutes or until lentils are tender. Season with salt and black pepper. Stir in 2 cups of the corn; cook 10 minutes more, stirring occasionally.

3. Using an immersion blender or food processor, blend soup until smooth. Just before serving, in a small saucepan heat chili oil over medium heat. Add remaining 1 cup corn to oil. Cook until corn is golden, 3 to 4 minutes. To serve, top soup with toasted corn, and, if desired, sour cream. Makes 6 servings.

PER SERVING *325 cal., 8 g fat (1 g sat. fat), 0 mg chol., 928 mg sodium, 50 g carb., 8 g fiber, 17 g pro.*

**MUSHROOM BISQUE
WITH LEMON
GREMOLATA**

MUSHROOM BISQUE WITH LEMON GREMOLATA

PREP 30 minutes
SLOW COOK 6 hours (low) or 3 hours (high) plus 30 minutes (high)

16 oz. fresh cremini mushrooms, halved
8   oz. fresh shiitake mushrooms, stemmed and halved
2   Tbsp. olive oil
½   tsp. salt
¼   tsp. black pepper
2½ cups vegetable broth or reduced-sodium chicken broth
1   cup chopped onion
¼   cup dry sherry or white wine
4   cloves garlic, minced

2   Tbsp. all-purpose flour
2   Tbsp. butter, softened
1   8-oz. carton crème fraîche
1   Tbsp. chopped fresh dill
1½ tsp. lemon zest

1. Place mushrooms in a 3½- or 4-quart slow cooker. Drizzle with oil and sprinkle with salt and pepper; toss to coat. Stir in broth, onion, sherry, and garlic. Cover and cook on low 6 to 7 hours or high 3 to 3½ hours.

2. Using an immersion blender, blend mushroom mixture until nearly smooth, leaving some coarse mushroom pieces. (Or cool slightly and transfer, half at a time, to a food processor or blender. Cover and process or blend until nearly smooth.)

CORN-LENTIL
CHOWDER

Holiday Party

Kick off entertaining season with this selection of savory and sweet appetizers. Choose from flatbread, sliders, wings, meatballs, sparkling beverages, and so much more.

BRUSSELS SPROUTS
AND GOAT CHEESE
FLATBREAD, PAGE 34

27

PROSCIUTTO-WRAPPED
SCALLOPS WITH ROASTED
RED PEPPER AÏOLI

PROSCIUTTO-WRAPPED SCALLOPS WITH ROASTED RED PEPPER AÏOLI

PREP 35 minutes
BROIL 6 minutes
STAND 30 minutes

- 10 fresh or frozen sea scallops
- 10 thin slices prosciutto, halved lengthwise, or 10 slices center-cut bacon, halved crosswise
- 20 medium fresh basil leaves
Freshly ground black pepper
- 1 recipe Roasted Red Pepper Aïoli
Snipped fresh basil (optional)

1. Thaw scallops, if frozen. Soak twenty 6-inch wooden skewers in water at least 30 minutes.
2. Meanwhile, place an oven rack 4 to 5 inches from the broiler element. Preheat broiler. Lightly grease the rack of a broiler pan (do not preheat). Rinse scallops; pat dry with paper towels. Cut scallops in half.
3. Lay prosciutto on a large cutting board. Top with a basil leaf and a scallop half. Starting from a short end, wrap prosciutto around scallop. Insert a skewer. Sprinkle with pepper.
4. Place kabobs on prepared pan. Broil 6 to 8 minutes or until scallops are opaque and prosciutto is crisp, turning once.
5. Serve kabobs with Roasted Red Pepper Aïoli for dipping. If desired, top aïoli with snipped fresh basil. Makes 20 servings.
Roasted Red Pepper Aïoli In a blender or food processor combine ½ cup bottled roasted red sweet peppers, drained, and 2 cloves garlic, cut up. Cover and blend until nearly smooth. Add ⅓ cup mayonnaise. Cover and blend until smooth. With blender or processor running, gradually add 2 tablespoons olive oil through opening in lid or feed tube, blending until smooth. Transfer aïoli to a bowl. Season with ⅛ teaspoon salt and a dash freshly ground black pepper. Cover and chill until ready to serve.
Make Ahead Prepare aïoli as directed. Cover and chill up to 2 days. Thin with a little water, if desired.
PER SERVING 92 cal., 7 g fat (1 g sat. fat), 11 mg chol., 231 mg sodium, 1 g carb., 0 g fiber, 7 g pro.

SCOTCH EGGS

SCOTCH EGGS

PREP 30 minutes
BAKE 30 minutes at 350°F

- ⅓ cup finely chopped onion
- 1 Tbsp. snipped fresh chives
- 1 tsp. dried sage, crushed
- ¾ tsp. sea salt
- ¾ tsp. black pepper
- ½ tsp. dried thyme, crushed
- 1 lb. ground pork
- 6 eggs, hard-cooked and peeled*
- ⅓ cup almond meal
- 2 Tbsp. sesame seeds and/or poppy seeds
- ½ cup mayonnaise
- 1 tsp. ground ancho or chipotle chile pepper
- 1 tsp. fresh lime juice
- 1 small clove garlic, minced
- 6 cups arugula or fresh spinach

1. Preheat oven to 350°F. Line a shallow baking pan with foil. In a medium bowl combine first six ingredients (through thyme). Add ground pork; mix well.
2. Divide meat mixture into six portions. Flatten into thin patties then fold around eggs, sealing and smoothing edges to completely enclose.
3. In a shallow dish combine almond meal and sesame seeds. Roll eggs in almond mixture to coat; place in prepared baking pan. Bake 30 minutes or until meat is no longer pink.
4. Meanwhile, for spicy mayonnaise, in a small bowl combine mayonnaise, ground ancho chile pepper, lime juice, and garlic. Cover and chill until serving. Halve Scotch Eggs; serve on arugula with spicy mayonnaise. Makes 6 servings.
*Tip To hard-cook eggs, place them in a single layer in a large saucepan. Add enough cold water to cover eggs by 1 inch. Bring to a full rolling boil over high heat; remove from heat. Cover and let stand 15 minutes; drain. Place eggs in ice water to cool; drain. To peel, gently tap each egg on countertop. Roll egg between the palms of your hands. Peel off eggshell, starting at large end.
PER SERVING 434 cal., 36 g fat (8 g sat. fat), 250 mg chol., 474 mg sodium, 5 g carb., 2 g fiber, 23 g pro.

**TANDOORI
CHICKEN WINGS**

POTATO PANCAKES WITH WHITE CHEDDAR AND GREEN CHILES

START TO FINISH 35 minutes

1	8-oz. carton sour cream or crème fraîche
1	Tbsp. finely chopped shallot
1	Tbsp. lime juice
1	tsp. finely chopped fresh cilantro
½	tsp. ground cumin
2	eggs, lightly beaten
¼	cup all-purpose flour
¼	tsp. salt
⅛	tsp. black pepper
1	cup shredded sharp white cheddar cheese (4 oz.)
1	4-oz. can diced green chile peppers, drained
1	lb. russet potatoes
1	small yellow onion
¼	cup canola oil
	Thinly sliced fresh serrano chile peppers* (optional)

1. For topping, in a small bowl combine first five ingredients (through cumin). Cover and chill until ready to serve.
2. In a medium bowl combine eggs, flour, salt, and black pepper. Stir in cheese and canned chile peppers.
3. Peel potatoes. Using a handheld grater or food processor, coarsely shred potatoes. Press shredded potatoes between paper towels to remove excess moisture. Coarsely shred onion; press between paper towels. Stir shredded potatoes and onion into egg mixture.
4. In a large heavy nonstick skillet heat 2 tablespoons of the oil over medium-high heat. Drop potato mixture by level tablespoons into hot oil; spread if needed. Cook 4 minutes or until edges are golden, turning once. Remove from skillet; cover and keep warm. Repeat with remaining 2 tablespoons oil and potato mixture. Serve warm pancakes with topping and, if desired, sprinkle with serrano peppers and additional cilantro. Makes 15 servings.
*Tip Chile peppers contain oils that can irritate skin and eyes. Wear plastic or rubber gloves when working with them.
PER SERVING *133 cal., 10 g fat (4 g sat. fat), 41 mg chol., 146 mg sodium, 8 g carb., 1 g fiber, 4 g pro.*

TANDOORI CHICKEN WINGS

PREP 45 minutes
MARINATE 4 hours
BAKE 35 minutes at 400°F per batch
BROIL 6 minutes per batch

1	8-oz. can tomato sauce
1	6-oz. carton plain low-fat yogurt
1	medium onion, cut into wedges
1	Tbsp. ground coriander
4	cloves garlic, coarsely chopped
2	tsp. chopped fresh ginger
1½	tsp. salt
1	tsp. cumin seeds
1	tsp. garam masala
1	tsp. paprika
½	to 1 tsp. cayenne pepper (optional)
½	tsp. ground turmeric
2	whole cloves
5	lb. chicken wing drummettes (50)
1	recipe Raita
	Snipped fresh parsley (optional)

1. For masala, in a blender or food processor combine all ingredients except chicken, Raita, and parsley. Cover and blend or process to form a smooth paste.
2. Place chicken drummettes in a resealable plastic bag set in a shallow dish. Pour masala over chicken. Seal bag; turn to coat chicken. Marinate in refrigerator 4 to 24 hours.
3. Preheat oven to 400°F. Drain chicken; discard tandoori masala. In batches, arrange chicken in a single layer on the rack of a large broiler pan. Bake 35 minutes. Remove chicken from oven. Preheat broiler. Broil chicken 4 to 5 inches from heat 6 to 8 minutes or until no longer pink and pieces just start to blacken, turning once.
4. Serve chicken with Raita and, if desired, sprinkle with parsley. Makes 16 servings.
Raita In a bowl combine one 6-ounce carton plain low-fat yogurt, ½ cup finely chopped tomato, ½ cup seeded and finely chopped cucumber, 1 tablespoon snipped fresh parsley, and 2 cloves garlic, minced.
PER SERVING *275 cal., 20 g fat (6 g sat. fat), 71 mg chol., 325 mg sodium, 3 g carb., 0 g fiber, 19 g pro.*

POTATO
PANCAKES WITH
WHITE CHEDDAR
AND GREEN
CHILES

BRAT MEATBALLS
WITH BEER-
MUSTARD SAUCE

BUFFALO
CHICKEN
TOTCHOS

ITALIAN ROAST
BEEF SLIDER
MELTS

BRAT MEATBALLS WITH BEER-MUSTARD SAUCE

PREP 35 minutes
BAKE 25 minutes at 375°F
SLOW COOK 3 hours (low) or 1½ hours (high)

2 eggs
½ cup fine dry bread crumbs
½ cup finely chopped onion
¼ cup milk
½ tsp. salt
½ tsp. black pepper
4 uncooked bratwurst links, casings removed
1 lb. ground beef
1 12-oz. bottle beer
⅓ cup coarse-ground mustard
¼ cup finely chopped onion

1. Preheat oven to 375°F. In a large bowl beat eggs with a fork. Stir in bread crumbs, onion, milk, salt, and pepper. Add bratwurst and ground beef; mix well. Shape into 36 meatballs. Place meatballs on a 15×10-inch baking pan. Bake 25 to 30 minutes or until meatballs are cooked through (160°F). Drain off fat.
2. Place meatballs in a 3½- or 4-quart slow cooker. For sauce, in a bowl stir together beer, mustard, and onion; pour over meatballs.
3. Cover and cook on low 3 to 4 hours or high 1½ to 2 hours. Keep warm, covered, on warm setting up to 2 hours. Makes 18 servings.
PER SERVING 154 cal., 10 g fat (4 g sat. fat), 52 mg chol., 370 mg sodium, 4 g carb., 0 g fiber, 8 g pro.

BUFFALO CHICKEN TOTCHOS

PREP 10 minutes
BAKE 35 minutes at 450°F

1 32-oz. pkg. frozen fried potato nuggets
¾ cup cayenne pepper sauce, such as Frank's Red Hot
¼ cup butter
½ tsp. garlic powder
4 cups shredded cooked chicken
2 cups shredded Colby and Monterey Jack cheese (8 oz.)
1 cup crumbled blue cheese (4 oz.)
1 cup finely chopped celery
2 Tbsp. thinly sliced green onion
½ cup blue cheese salad dressing

1. Preheat oven to 450°F. Spread potatoes in a 15×10-inch baking pan. Bake 30 minutes. Meanwhile, in a large saucepan combine cayenne pepper sauce, butter, and garlic powder. Heat over low just until butter is melted, stirring occasionally. Remove from heat. Stir in chicken.
2. Spoon chicken mixture over potatoes. Top with cheeses. Bake 5 minutes or until cheeses are melted.
3. Top with celery and green onion. Drizzle with blue cheese dressing and, if desired, additional cayenne pepper sauce. Makes 12 servings.
PER SERVING 416 cal., 28 g fat (11 g sat. fat), 79 mg chol., 1,107 mg sodium, 20 g carb., 2 g fiber, 22 g pro.

ITALIAN ROAST BEEF SLIDER MELTS

PREP 10 minutes
BAKE 25 minutes at 350°F

12 3-inch sourdough rolls
12 oz. thinly sliced deli-style roast beef
1½ cups chopped pickled mixed vegetables (giardiniera)
6 oz. thinly sliced provolone or mozzarella cheese
1 8-oz. tub cream cheese spread with garden vegetables
¼ cup olive oil
2 cloves garlic, minced
1 tsp. dried Italian seasoning, crushed
½ tsp. crushed red pepper

1. Preheat oven to 350°F. Arrange bottoms of rolls in a 13×9-inch baking pan or dish. Layer roll bottoms with roast beef, pickled mixed vegetables, and provolone. Spread cut sides of roll tops with cream cheese; place on cheese.
2. In a bowl combine oil, garlic, Italian seasoning, and crushed red pepper. Drizzle over rolls. Cover pan with foil.
3. Bake 15 minutes. Remove foil; bake 10 to 15 minutes more or until cheese is melted and roll tops are light brown. Makes 12 servings.
Make Ahead Assemble sliders. Do not drizzle with olive oil mixture. Cover and refrigerate up to 8 hours. Drizzle then bake as directed.
PER SERVING 362 cal., 16 g fat (7 g sat. fat), 51 mg chol., 881 mg sodium, 35 g carb., 1 g fiber, 19 g pro.

CHEESEBURGER
SLIDER DIP

PIMIENTO CHEESE PULL-APART CHRISTMAS TREE

PREP 30 minutes
BAKE 20 minutes at 400°F

8	oz. sharp white cheddar cheese, shredded (2 cups)
1	8-oz. pkg. cream cheese, cubed and softened
⅛	tsp. garlic powder
⅛	tsp. onion powder
⅛	tsp. black pepper
½	4-oz. jar diced pimientos, drained
1	small jalapeño, seeded and finely chopped (tip, page 30)
2	11-oz. tubes refrigerated thin pizza crust
1	large egg
	Fresh thyme

1. In a large bowl stir together the first five ingredients (through black pepper). Stir in pimientos and jalapeño. Set aside.
2. Preheat oven to 400°F. Adjust oven rack to lower third of oven. Lightly dust two large sheets of parchment paper with flour. One at a time, unroll each package of dough on a sheet of parchment. Pat to a 15×12-inch rectangle. To shape a tree, cut from the corners of one narrow side toward the center top, forming one large center triangle. Remove and set aside the two long narrow triangles at each side.
3. Transfer one tree-shape dough along with parchment to a large baking sheet. Spread the cheese mixture on the dough, leaving a ½ inch border around all sides. Carefully invert the second tree-shape dough onto cheese-covered dough. Remove parchment, then press dough edges together to seal.
4. To shape tree limbs, begin 2 inches from tree top and snip diagonally upward along long sides of tree, snipping at 1½-inch intervals. To shape a tree trunk to fit the center of tree, lightly twist together pairs of reserved side pieces of dough; stack and arrange twists in center of tree.
5. In a small bowl whisk together egg and 1 tablespoon water. Lightly brush on tree.
6. Bake 20 to 25 minutes or until golden brown (some cheese may ooze out). Remove from oven. Sprinkle with additional chopped pimiento and fresh thyme. Serve warm. Makes 12 servings.
PER SERVING *299 cal., 17 g fat (9 g sat. fat), 39 mg chol., 482 mg sodium, 26 g carb., 1 g fiber, 9 g pro.*

CHEESEBURGER SLIDER DIP

PREP 20 minutes
SLOW COOK 3 hours (low) or 1½ hours (high)

1	lb. lean ground beef
1	cup chopped onion
1	clove garlic, minced
12	oz. process cheese food, such as Velveeta, cut up
⅔	cup chopped tomato
3	Tbsp. tomato paste
3	Tbsp. yellow mustard
2	tsp. Worcestershire sauce
2	to 3 Tbsp. milk (optional)
	Pickle slices (optional)
	French-fried crinkle-cut potatoes, sweet potato fries, and/or thick potato chips

1. In a large skillet cook ground beef, onion, and garlic over medium-high heat until meat is browned. Drain off fat.
2. In a 1½- or 2-quart slow cooker combine meat mixture, cheese, tomato, tomato paste, mustard, and Worcestershire sauce. Cover and cook on low 3 to 4 hours or high 1½ to 2 hours. If necessary, stir in milk to reach desired consistency.
3. Serve immediately or keep warm, covered, on warm or low up to 2 hours, stirring occasionally. If desired, top with pickle slices. Serve with potatoes, fries, and/or chips. Makes 16 servings .
PER SERVING *125 cal., 8 g fat (4 g sat. fat), 35 mg chol., 401 mg sodium, 4 g carb., 1 g fiber, 10 g pro.*

BRUSSELS SPROUTS AND GOAT CHEESE FLATBREAD

PREP 10 minutes
BAKE 4 minutes at 425°F

1	7-inch thin artisan pizza crust
1	oz. soft goat cheese (chèvre)
½	cup thinly sliced Brussels sprouts
3	Tbsp. snipped dried apricots
2	Tbsp. chopped walnuts, toasted*
½	tsp. honey
½	tsp. lime zest

1. Preheat oven to 425°F. Bake crust on oven rack 4 to 6 minutes or until golden and crisp.
2. Spread crust with cheese. Top with sprouts, apricots, and nuts. Drizzle with honey and lime zest. Makes 8 servings.
*Tip To toast a small amount of nuts, heat in a skillet over medium-low heat for 3 to 5 minutes or until fragrant and lightly browned.
PER SERVING *190 cal., 8 g fat (3 g sat. fat), 7 mg chol., 266 mg sodium, 23 g carb., 3 g fiber, 7 g pro.*

PIMIENTO CHEESE
PULL-APART
CHRISTMAS TREE

CRANBERRY-NUT
STICKS

CRANBERRY-NUT STICKS

PREP 25 minutes
STAND 15 minutes
BAKE 38 minutes at 350°F

1   16.5-oz. pkg. refrigerated sugar cookie dough
1   tsp. ground ginger
½   tsp. ground cinnamon
¼   tsp. ground cloves
2   eggs
1   cup walnuts, chopped
½   cup packed brown sugar
½   cup molasses
½   cup fresh cranberries, chopped
4   oz. white baking chocolate, chopped

1. Preheat oven to 350°F. Line a 13×9-inch baking pan with foil, extending foil over edges of pan; set aside. Place cookie dough in a large bowl; let stand 15 minutes. Knead in the ginger, cinnamon, and cloves. Press dough into prepared pan. Bake 20 minutes.
2. Meanwhile, for filling, in a medium bowl stir together the eggs, walnuts, brown sugar, molasses, and cranberries. Pour over baked crust; spread evenly. Bake 18 to 20 minutes or until filling is set. Cool in pan on a wire rack.
3. In a small saucepan melt white baking chocolate over low heat until smooth, stirring constantly. Drizzle over uncut bars. Let stand until set. Use foil to lift bars out of pan. Transfer to a cutting board. Cut into narrow bars. Makes 30 servings.
PER SERVING *150 cal., 7 g fat (2 g sat. fat), 18 mg chol., 78 mg sodium, 20 g carb., 0 g fiber, 2 g pro.*

CHILE PECANS

CHILE PECANS

PREP 15 minutes
BAKE 45 minutes at 250°F

2   cups pecan halves
2   Tbsp. maple syrup or coffee
     liqueur
4   tsp. vegetable oil
2   Tbsp. sugar
2   Tbsp. ground ancho, Chimayo, or
     pasilla chile pepper

1. Preheat oven to 250°F. Line a 13×9-inch
baking pan with foil; set aside. In a
medium bowl combine pecan halves,
syrup and oil. Stir in sugar and chile
pepper. Spread in prepared pan.
2. Bake, uncovered, 45 minutes, stirring
twice. Spread on a large piece of foil to
cool. Makes 10 servings.
PER SERVING *192 cal., 18 g fat (2 g sat.
fat), 0 mg chol., 16 mg sodium, 8 g carb.,
3 g fiber, 2 g pro.*

COFFEE SHAKE SHOTS

START TO FINISH 15 minutes

1   qt. coffee-flavor ice cream
     Chocolate syrup
½   to 1 cup milk
6   Tbsp. coffee liqueur
     Chocolate curls or shavings
     (optional)

1. Let ice cream stand at room
temperature 5 minutes. Meanwhile,
drizzle a little chocolate syrup in eight
2- to 3-ounce glasses; set aside.

2. In a blender combine ice cream,
milk, and liqueur. Cover and blend on
medium-high until thick and smooth.
Spoon ice cream mixture into glasses. If
desired, top each serving with chocolate
curls. Makes 8 servings.
Tip If you don't find coffee-flavor ice
cream, dissolve 1 tablespoon regular or
decaffeinated instant coffee crystals in
3 tablespoons coffee liqueur and use
vanilla ice cream.
PER SERVING *136 cal., 3 g fat (2 g
sat. fat), 11 mg chol., 44 mg sodium,
22 g carb., 0 g fiber, 3 g pro.*

CITRUS SIDECAR

CITRUS SIDECAR

START TO FINISH 10 minutes

    Superfine granulated sugar
    (optional)
½ cup brandy
½ cup fresh orange juice or lemon
    juice
⅓ cup orange liqueur (Cointreau,
    Triple Sec, or Grand Marnier
    Ice cubes
3 orange or lemon slices

1. If desired, wet the rims of three glasses
with water; dip glass rims in sugar.
If desired, chill glasses. In a cocktail
shaker combine brandy, orange juice,
and orange liqueur. Add 1 cup ice
cubes; cover and shake until combined
and very cold. Strain into three chilled
glasses or three glasses filled with
additional ice cubes. Add orange
wedges. Makes 3 servings.
PER SERVING *190 cal., 0 g fat, 0 mg chol.,
1 mg sodium, 14 g carb., 0 g fiber, 0 g pro.*

PARTY PUNCH

PREP 15 minutes
CHILL 4 hours

4 cups water
1 12-oz. can frozen juice
    concentrate, thawed (cranberry,
    lemonade, limeade, orange, or
    pineapple)
1 cup sugar
2½ cups juice blend, chilled
    (cranberry-apple, pineapple-
    orange-banana, pink grapefruit,
    pomegranate, raspberry, or
    strawberry)
1 2-liter bottle carbonated
    beverage, chilled (cream soda,
    ginger ale, lemon-lime, orange, or
    strawberry)
1 cup citrus fruit slices, berries,
    sherbet, or sorbet (optional)

1. In a large pitcher or bowl combine the
water and frozen juice concentrate. Add
sugar; stir until dissolved. Cover and chill
at least 4 hours.
2. To serve, pour juice mixture into an
extra-large punch bowl. Stir in juice blend.
Slowly stir in carbonated beverage. If
desired, add fruit. Makes 16 servings.
PER SERVING *174 cal., 0 g fat, 0 mg chol.,
20 mg sodium, 44 g carb., 1 g fiber,
1 g pro.*

PARTY PUNCH

**TROPICAL FRUIT WITH
HONEY-LIME SYRUP,
PAGE 54**

Brunch Buffet

Make serving easy. Set out a brunch buffet for guests to browse and help themselves. Choose from this collection of recipes that appeals to many tastes.

STICKY APPLE-
CINNAMON ROLLS,
PAGE 46

SOUR CREAM SWIRL
COFFEE CAKE

SOUR CREAM SWIRL COFFEE CAKE

PREP 25 minutes
BAKE 45 minutes at 350°F
COOL 20 minutes

2   cups granulated sugar
1   cup butter, softened
2   eggs
1   8-oz. carton sour cream
½   tsp. vanilla
2   cups all-purpose flour
1   tsp. baking powder
¼   tsp. salt
⅔   cup chopped pecans
2   Tbsp. packed brown sugar
1½   tsp. ground cinnamon
     Sifted powdered sugar

1. Preheat oven to 350°F. Grease and flour a 10-inch fluted tube pan. Set aside.
2. In a large bowl beat sugar and butter with a mixer on medium until mixture is light and fluffy. Add eggs; beat well. Beat in sour cream and vanilla just until combined.
3. In a small bowl combine flour, baking powder, and salt. Beat into creamed mixture until combined. Pour half the batter into prepared pan.
4. In a small bowl stir together pecans, brown sugar, and cinnamon. Sprinkle ½ cup nut mixture on batter in pan. Carefully spread remaining batter on nut mixture. Sprinkle with remaining nut mixture; press lightly into batter.
5. Bake 45 to 50 minutes or until a wooden toothpick inserted near center comes out clean.
6. Cool cake in pan on a wire rack 5 minutes. Invert cake onto a serving plate. Cool 15 minutes more. Dust with powdered sugar. Serve warm or cool. Makes 12 servings.
PER SERVING *444 cal., 24 g fat (13 g sat. fat), 82 mg chol., 242 mg sodium, 54 g carb., 1 g fiber, 4 g pro.*

BLUEBERRY-NUT STREUSEL COFFEE CAKE

BLUEBERRY-NUT STREUSEL COFFEE CAKE

PREP 30 minutes
BAKE 35 minutes at 350°F
COOL 1 hour

1½   cups packed brown sugar
1   cup coarsely chopped walnuts
2   tsp. ground cinnamon
1   8-oz. carton sour cream
1   tsp. baking soda
¾   cup granulated sugar
½   cup butter, softened
1   tsp. vanilla
3   eggs
2   cups all-purpose flour
1½   tsp. baking powder
2   cups fresh or frozen blueberries, thawed
¾   cup powdered sugar
1   Tbsp. milk
½   tsp. vanilla

1. Preheat oven to 350°F. For topping, in a medium bowl combine brown sugar, nuts, and cinnamon. In small bowl stir together sour cream and baking soda (mixture will foam). Grease a 10-inch tube pan.
2. In a large bowl beat granulated sugar and softened butter with a mixer on medium 2 minutes. Add vanilla and eggs, one at a time, beating well after each addition. Beat in flour and baking powder until well combined. Add sour cream mixture; beat until well combined.
3. Spread half the batter in the prepared pan. Sprinkle blueberries and all but 1 cup of the topping over the batter. Spread remaining batter over topping. Sprinkle remaining topping over batter.
4. Bake 35 to 40 minutes or until a toothpick inserted near center comes out clean. Cool 1 hour before inverting cake onto a cake plate.
5. For powdered sugar icing, in a small bowl combine powdered sugar, milk, and vanilla. Stir in enough additional milk, 1 teaspoon at a time, to make drizzling consistency. Drizzle cooled cake with icing. Makes 16 servings.
PER SERVING *347 cal., 14 g fat (6 g sat. fat), 58 mg chol., 195 mg sodium, 52 g carb., 2 g fiber, 4 g pro.*

CARAMEL-BANANA MUFFINS

PREP 25 minutes
BAKE 18 minutes at 375°F
COOL 5 minutes

1¼ cups all-purpose flour
¾ tsp. baking powder
¼ tsp. baking soda
¼ tsp. salt
½ cup chopped pecans
2 Tbsp. sugar
1 tsp. ground cinnamon
1 3-oz. pkg. cream cheese, softened
¼ cup butter, softened
⅔ cup sugar
1 egg
1 medium banana, mashed (½ cup)
1 tsp. vanilla
2 Tbsp. caramel-flavor ice cream topping
1 medium banana, thinly sliced (optional)
1 Tbsp. butter, melted

1. Preheat oven to 375°F. Line twelve 2½-inch muffin cups with paper bake cups. In a medium bowl stir together the first four ingredients (through salt); set aside. In a small bowl stir together pecans, 2 tablespoons sugar, and cinnamon; set aside.
2. In a bowl beat cream cheese, ¼ cup softened butter, and ⅔ cup sugar with a mixer on medium until well combined. Add egg; beat well. Beat in mashed banana and vanilla until combined. Add flour mixture, beating on low just until moistened (batter will be lumpy). Stir in ¼ cup of the pecan mixture.
3. Spoon half the batter into prepared muffin cups (1 rounded tablespoon for each 2½-inch muffin cup). Drizzle ½ teaspoon caramel topping over batter. Top with remaining batter. If desired, top with two banana slices. Drizzle with melted butter and sprinkle with remaining pecan mixture.
4. Bake 18 to 20 minutes or until a toothpick inserted in centers comes out clean. Cool in pan on a wire rack 5 minutes. Remove from pan. Serve warm and, if desired, drizzle with additional caramel topping and chopped pecans. Makes 12 servings.
PER SERVING 222 cal., 11 g fat (5 g sat. fat), 38 mg chol., 172 mg sodium, 29 g carb., 1 g fiber, 3 g pro.

CHOCOLATE-BANANA FRENCH TOAST BAKE

PREP 20 minutes
CHILL 2 hours
BAKE 40 minutes at 375°F

8 ½-inch slices soft French bread
½ cup chocolate-hazelnut spread
1½ cups sliced bananas
4 eggs, lightly beaten
1 cup milk
⅓ cup half-and-half
  Maple syrup, warmed
  Fresh raspberries (optional)

1. Grease a 2-quart rectangular baking dish. Spread half the bread slices with chocolate-hazelnut spread. Top with bananas and remaining bread slices. Cut sandwiches into quarters. Place, cut sides up, in prepared baking dish.
2. In a medium bowl combine eggs, milk, and half-and-half. Pour egg mixture over sandwich pieces. Cover and chill 2 to 24 hours.
3. Preheat oven to 375°F. Bake, uncovered, 40 to 45 minutes or until golden and a knife inserted near center comes out clean. Serve with warm maple syrup, and top with fresh raspberries if desired. Makes 6 servings.
PER SERVING 382 cal., 14 g fat (5 g sat. fat), 132 mg chol., 274 mg sodium, 53 g carb., 2 g fiber, 10 g pro.

CARAMEL-BANANA MUFFINS

CHOCOLATE-
BANANA FRENCH
TOAST BAKE

STICKY APPLE-CINNAMON ROLLS

PREP 40 minutes
RISE 1 hour 30 minutes
BAKE 40 minutes at 350°F

6¼ to 6¾ cups all-purpose flour
2   pkg. active dry yeast
2   cups milk
¼   cup granulated sugar
¼   cup butter
1½ tsp. salt
1   egg
½   cup packed brown sugar
½   cup granulated sugar
¼   cup all-purpose flour
1   Tbsp. ground cinnamon
½   cup butter
2   cups finely chopped peeled apple
1   cup chopped pecans
1   recipe Caramel Syrup

1. In a large bowl combine 2½ cups of flour and the yeast. Set aside.
2. In a medium saucepan heat and stir milk, ¼ cup granulated sugar, ¼ cup butter, and salt just until warm (120°F to 130°F) and butter is almost melted.

Add milk mixture to flour mixture. Then add egg. Beat with a mixer on low 30 seconds. Beat on high 3 minutes. Stir in as much remaining flour as you can.
3. Turn dough out onto a lightly floured surface. Knead in enough remaining flour to make a moderately soft dough that's smooth and elastic (3 to 5 minutes total). Shape dough into a ball. Place dough in lightly greased bowl, turning once to grease surface of dough. Cover; let rise in a warm place until doubled (45 to 60 minutes).
4. For filling, in a small bowl combine ½ cup brown sugar, ½ cup granulated sugar, ¼ cup flour, and cinnamon. Cut in ½ cup butter until mixture resembles coarse crumbs.
5. Punch dough down. Turn dough out onto a lightly floured surface. Cover and let rest 10 minutes. Grease a 13×9-inch baking pan; set aside.
6. Roll dough into a 24×16-inch rectangle. Sprinkle with filling, apple, and nuts. Roll up jelly-roll style, from long side. Pinch to seal edge.
7. Prepare Caramel Syrup. Pour into baking pan. Cut dough, crosswise,

into 12 rolls. Place, cut sides down, in prepared pan. Cover and let rolls rise until nearly doubled (about 45 minutes).
8. Preheat oven to 350°F. Bake, uncovered, 40 minutes or until lightly browned and rolls sound hollow when lightly tapped. (Place baking sheet under baking pan to catch any drips.) Invert onto serving plate while warm. Makes 12 servings.
Caramel Syrup In a small saucepan melt ½ cup butter; stir in 1 cup packed brown sugar and ¼ cup corn syrup. Cook and stir until sugar is melted. Remove from heat.
PER SERVING 687 cal., 29 g fat (14 g sat. fat), 76 mg chol., 544 mg sodium, 100 g carb., 4 g fiber, 10 g pro.

CREAMY BUTTER-PECAN CINNAMON ROLLS WITH CHOCOLATE

PREP 25 minutes
RISE 45 minutes
BAKE 40 minutes at 375°F
COOL 5 minutes

1   cup sifted powdered sugar
⅓   cup heavy cream
1   cup coarsely chopped pecans
½   cup packed brown sugar
1   Tbsp. ground cinnamon
2   tsp. all-purpose flour
2   14- to 16-oz. loaves frozen sweet roll or white bread dough, thawed
¼   cup butter or margarine, melted
½   cup semisweet chocolate pieces
½   cup chopped pecans

1. In a small bowl stir together powdered sugar and cream. Pour into a 13×9-inch baking dish; sprinkle with 1 cup coarsely chopped pecans.
2. In a small bowl stir together brown sugar, cinnamon, and flour; set aside.
3. On a lightly floured surface, roll each loaf into a 12×8-inch rectangle. Brush dough with melted butter; sprinkle with brown sugar mixture, chocolate pieces, and ½ cup chopped pecans. Roll up dough from a long side. Seal seams. Cut each roll crosswise into six pieces. Arrange pieces, cut side down, in prepared dish. Cover with a towel. Let rise in a warm place until nearly doubled (45 to 60 minutes). Break surface bubbles with a greased toothpick.

CREAMY BUTTER-PECAN CINNAMON ROLLS WITH CHOCOLATE

4. Preheat oven to 375°F. Bake 40 to 45 minutes or until sides of rolls are browned and center rolls do not appear doughy (do not underbake). If necessary, cover top with foil during last 15 to 20 minutes to prevent overbrowning. Cool in pan on a wire rack 5 minutes. Loosen edges; invert onto a serving platter. Serve warm. Makes 12 servings.

PER SERVING *443 cal., 22 g fat (8 g sat. fat), 58 mg chol., 167 mg sodium, 60 g carb., 3 g fiber, 7 g pro.*

SAUSAGE-APPLE DUTCH BABY

PREP 15 minutes
BAKE 15 minutes at 425°F

- 3 oz. fully cooked smoked chicken-apple sausage, thinly sliced
- 3½ Tbsp. butter
- 3 eggs
- ½ cup all-purpose flour
- ½ cup milk
- 1 Tbsp. granulated sugar
- ½ tsp. vanilla
- ¼ tsp. salt
- ¼ tsp. ground cinnamon
- 1 medium red cooking apple, cored and thinly sliced
- 2 Tbsp. brown sugar
- 2 Tbsp. pure maple syrup

1. Preheat oven to 425°F. In a 9-inch cast-iron or oven-going skillet cook sausage in 1½ tablespoons hot butter over medium heat until browned.
2. Meanwhile, in a medium bowl beat eggs well. Add flour, milk, granulated sugar, vanilla, salt, and cinnamon; whisk vigorously until smooth. Immediately pour batter into hot skillet over sausage. Transfer to oven; bake 15 minutes, or until browned and puffed.
3. While pancake bakes, melt remaining 2 tablespoons butter over medium-high heat. Add apple. Cook, stirring occasionally, 5 minutes or until apple is crisp-tender and lightly browned around edges. Add brown sugar and maple syrup. Cook 2 to 3 minutes, or until apple is tender. Serve Dutch Baby topped with apples. Makes 4 servings.

PER SERVING *349 cal., 17 g fat (9 g sat. fat), 189 mg chol., 457 mg sodium, 37 g carb., 2 g fiber, 11 g pro.*

STICKY APPLE-CINNAMON ROLLS

SAUSAGE-APPLE DUTCH BABY

MINI QUICHES

PREP 20 minutes
BAKE 13 minutes at 425°F
COOL 2 minutes

1 14.1-oz. pkg. rolled refrigerated unbaked piecrust (2 crusts)
2 eggs, lightly beaten
⅔ cup milk
¼ cup finely chopped green onions
¼ tsp. salt
¼ tsp. freshly ground black pepper
½ to 1 cup finely chopped or crumbled cooked meat and/or vegetable, such as bacon, ham, sausage, shrimp, spinach, broccoli, or red sweet pepper
¼ to ½ cup finely shredded or crumbled cheese

1. Preheat oven to 425°F. Let piecrust stand according to package directions.
2. Meanwhile, in a large glass measuring cup or medium bowl combine next five ingredients (through pepper).
3. Unroll piecrust. Using a 2½- or 3-inch round cutter, cut out pastry. Press pastry circles onto bottoms and up sides of twenty-four 1¾-inch muffin cups. Place a pinch of meat and/or vegetable and cheese into each pastry shell. Pour egg mixture over filling.
4. Bake 13 to 15 minutes or until filling is puffed and pastry is golden. Cool in muffin cups on a wire rack 2 minutes. Remove from muffin cups; serve warm. Makes 12 servings.
Make Ahead Prepare filling and press pastry circles into muffin cups as directed. Cover tightly with plastic wrap and chill 2 to 24 hours. To serve, assemble quiches and bake as directed.
PER SERVING *168 cal., 10 g fat (4 g sat. fat), 40 mg chol., 295 mg sodium, 17 g carb., 0 g fiber, 4 g pro.*

ORANGE-HONEY OVERNIGHT OATS

PREP 15 minutes
CHILL 8 hours

2 cups regular rolled oats
2 cups milk
1 cup plain low-fat Greek yogurt
½ cup unsweetened flaked coconut
2 Tbsp. honey
4 tsp. orange zest
1 tsp. snipped fresh thyme
Fresh berries (optional)

1. In a large bowl combine the first seven ingredients (through thyme). Cover and chill overnight.
2. Stir before serving. Top servings with berries (if using) and additional orange zest and/or thyme. Makes 6 servings.
PER SERVING *233 cal., 8 g fat (5 g sat. fat), 10 mg chol., 53 mg sodium, 33 g carb., 4 g fiber, 10 g pro.*

MINI QUICHES

ORANGE-HONEY
OVERNIGHT OATS

CHEESY CHORIZO
SHEET-PAN
FRITTATA

CHEESY CHORIZO SHEET-PAN FRITTATA

PREP 15 minutes
BAKE 10 minutes at 450°F

Nonstick cooking spray
8 oz. uncooked chorizo or bulk pork sausage
1 fresh poblano chile pepper, seeded and chopped*
½ cup chopped onion
1 15-oz. can reduced-sodium black beans, rinsed and drained
½ 12-oz. jar roasted red sweet peppers, drained and chopped
18 eggs
½ tsp. salt
¼ tsp. black pepper
¾ cup shredded Mexican cheese blend or cheddar cheese (3 oz.)
2 Tbsp. chopped fresh cilantro
Chopped tomatoes, sliced avocado, and/or fried tortilla strips (optional)

1. Preheat oven to 450°F. Generously coat a 15×10-inch baking pan with cooking spray.
2. In a large skillet cook sausage, poblano pepper, and onion over medium heat until sausage is browned; drain off fat. Stir in black beans and roasted peppers. Spread into prepared pan.
3. In a large bowl whisk together eggs, salt, and black pepper. Stir in cheese and cilantro. Pour egg mixture over sausage mixture. Bake 10 to 12 minutes or until set. If desired, top with tomatoes, avocado, and/or tortilla strips. Sprinkle with additional cheese and cilantro. Makes 12 servings.
*Tip Chile peppers contain oils that can irritate skin and eyes. Wear plastic or rubber gloves when working with them.
PER SERVING *211 cal., 12 g fat (4 g sat. fat), 305 mg chol., 481 mg sodium, 9 g carb., 2 g fiber, 16 g pro.*

SWEET POTATO HASH BROWN NESTS

SWEET POTATO HASH BROWN NESTS

PREP 25 minutes
COOK 7 minutes
BAKE 22 minutes at 400°F

1 tsp. vegetable oil
5 cups peeled and coarsely shredded sweet potatoes
1 cup finely chopped onion
1 tsp. garlic powder
1 tsp. dry mustard
½ tsp. salt
2 tsp. cornstarch
Nonstick cooking spray
4 thin slices prosciutto, halved crosswise
8 eggs
¼ cup shredded cheddar cheese
8 cherry tomatoes, diced or quartered
¼ cup thinly sliced green onions

1. Preheat oven to 400°F. In a large nonstick skillet heat oil over medium-high heat. Add next five ingredients (through salt). Cook 7 minutes or until potatoes begin to brown, stirring occasionally. Remove from heat. Stir in cornstarch.
2. Lightly coat eight 2½-inch muffin cups with cooking spray. Press about ¼ cup potato mixture onto bottom and up sides of muffin cups. Bake 10 minutes.
3. Line sweet potato cups with prosciutto. Break eggs, one at a time, into a small dish; slip eggs into sweet potato cups. Sprinkle with cheese. Bake 12 minutes or until egg whites are completely set and yolks are thickened. Remove from muffin cups. Top with tomatoes and green onions. Makes 8 servings.
PER SERVING *172 cal., 7 g fat (3 g sat. fat), 192 mg chol., 398 mg sodium, 16 g carb., 2 g fiber, 11 g pro.*

BUTTERNUT SQUASH MAC AND CHEESE

PREP 15 minutes
COOK 40 minutes
BAKE 14 minutes at 425°F
COOL 5 minutes

12 oz. dried rigatoni
1½ lb. butternut squash, peeled, seeded, cut into chunks (3½ cups)
2¾ cups milk
¼ cup all-purpose flour
8 oz. smoked Gruyère cheese, shredded (2 cups)
8 slices bacon
2 small sweet onions, coarsely chopped
3 oz. sourdough bread (1½ to 2 slices)
2 Tbsp. butter, melted
Fresh Italian parsley

1. Preheat oven to 425°F. Lightly butter a 3-quart oval or rectangular baking dish. Cook pasta according to package directions. Drain; transfer to a large bowl.

2. Meanwhile, in a large saucepan combine the squash and 2½ cups of the milk over medium-high heat. Bring to boiling; reduce heat to medium. Simmer until squash is tender when pierced with a fork, 18 to 20 minutes. Stir together remaining ¼ cup milk and flour; stir into squash mixture. Bring to boiling; cook until thickened, 2 to 3 minutes. Stir in 1½ cups of the cheese until melted; keep warm.

3. In an extra-large skillet cook bacon until crisp; transfer to paper towels to drain. Reserve 2 tablespoons bacon drippings in skillet. Return skillet to heat; add onions. Cover and cook over low heat, stirring occasionally, 10 minutes. Uncover and increase medium-heat to high. Cook 4 to 6 minutes more, stirring, until onions are golden. Crumble the bacon.

4. Add squash mixture, onions, and bacon to bowl with pasta; toss to combine. Transfer to prepared baking dish.

5. Place bread in a food processor and pulse two or three times to form large coarse crumbs (about 2 cups). Transfer to a small bowl; stir in melted butter. Sprinkle remaining cheese and bread crumbs over mac and cheese. Bake 14 to 15 minutes or until top is browned. Cool 5 minutes. Sprinkle with parsley. Makes 10 servings.

PER SERVING *411 cal., 17 g fat (9 g sat. fat), 47 mg chol., 401 mg sodium, 46 g carb., 5 g fiber, 18 g pro.*

BRUSSELS SPROUTS SKILLET CASSEROLE WITH PANCETTA

PREP 30 minutes
BAKE 15 minutes at 400°F

1¼ lb. Brussels sprouts, trimmed and coarsely chopped
1 cup chopped carrots
3 oz. pancetta or 8 slices bacon, chopped

BUTTERNUT SQUASH MAC AND CHEESE

BRUSSELS SPROUTS SKILLET CASSEROLE WITH PANCETTA

¼ cup finely chopped shallots or
   ½ cup chopped onion
1 Tbsp. butter
3 cloves garlic, minced
1 Tbsp. all-purpose flour
1 cup finely shredded Asiago or
   Parmesan cheese (4 oz.)
½ tsp. salt
½ tsp. black pepper
1 cup heavy cream
1 Tbsp. coarse ground mustard
   Dash crushed red pepper
½ cup panko bread crumbs or other
   coarse bread crumbs

1. Preheat oven to 400°F. In a large
saucepan cook Brussels sprouts and
carrots in lightly salted boiling water
5 to 6 minutes or until tender; drain well.
Return vegetables to saucepan.
2. Meanwhile, in a large oven-going
skillet cook pancetta over medium
heat until crisp. Using a slotted spoon,
transfer pancetta to paper towels to
drain; reserve drippings in skillet. Add
shallots, butter, and garlic to drippings;
cook and stir 30 seconds. Stir in flour.
Remove from heat. Stir in Brussels
sprouts and carrots, pancetta, ½ cup of
the cheese, salt, and black pepper.
3. In a small bowl stir together cream,
mustard, and crushed red pepper. Pour
over Brussels sprouts mixture. In another
small bowl stir together the remaining
½ cup cheese and panko. Sprinkle over
Brussels sprouts mixture.
4. Bake, uncovered, 15 to 20 minutes
or until bubbly and topping is golden.
Makes 8 servings.
PER SERVING *274 cal., 21 g fat (12 g sat.
fat), 69 mg chol., 603 mg sodium, 13 g
carb., 3 g fiber, 9 g pro.*

ZUCCHINI RIBBONS, PASTA, AND ARUGULA

START TO FINISH 30 minutes

6 oz. dried fettuccine
2 medium zucchini or yellow summer
   squash
1 lemon
3 cups arugula
¼ cup pepperoncini salad peppers
2 Tbsp. olive oil
1½ tsp. snipped fresh oregano
1 to 2 cloves garlic, minced
¼ tsp. salt
¼ tsp. black pepper
¼ cup chopped toasted almonds (tip,
   page 34)

ZUCCHINI RIBBONS,
PASTA, AND
ARUGULA

1. Cook fettuccine according to package
directions (do not drain). Meanwhile,
use a "Y" peeler, mandoline, or sharp
knife to slice zucchini lengthwise into thin
ribbons. Place zucchini in a colander;
pour undrained fettuccine over zucchini.
Immediately run cold water over
fettuccine mixture to cool; drain well.
2. Transfer fettuccine mixture to a large
bowl. Remove 1 teaspoon zest and
squeeze 1 tablespoon juice from lemon.

Add lemon zest and juice, arugula,
salad peppers, oil, oregano, and garlic
to fettuccine mixture; toss to combine.
Season to taste with salt and black
pepper. Top with toasted almonds.
Makes 8 servings.
PER SERVING *141 cal., 6 g fat (1 g sat.
fat), 0 mg chol., 191 mg sodium, 19 g
carb., 2 g fiber, 4 g pro.*

CUCUMBER, OLIVE, AND DILL SALAD

TROPICAL FRUIT WITH HONEY-LIME SYRUP

CUCUMBER, OLIVE, AND DILL SALAD

PREP 15 minutes
CHILL 2 hours

- ¼ cup red wine vinegar
- 2 Tbsp. fresh dill, chopped
- 1 Tbsp. canola oil
- 2 tsp. granulated sugar
- 1 tsp. salt
- 3 medium English cucumbers, thinly sliced
- ½ cup red onion, thinly sliced
- ½ cup sliced and pitted Kalamata olives

1. In a large bowl combine vinegar, chopped dill, oil, sugar, and salt. Stir in cucumbers, red onion, and olives. Cover; chill at least 2 hours before serving. Makes 12 servings.
PER SERVING 39 cal., 3 g fat (0 g sat. fat), 0 mg chol., 329 mg sodium, 3 g carb., 0 g fiber, 1 g pro.

TROPICAL FRUIT WITH HONEY-LIME SYRUP

START TO FINISH 30 minutes

- 1 small pineapple, peeled, cored, and cut into spears
- 2 medium papayas or large mangos, halved, seeded, peeled, and cut into 4-inch spears
- 5 cups strawberries, halved
- ½ cup lime juice
- ¼ cup honey
- 2 Tbsp. snipped fresh cilantro
- ½ tsp. ground ancho chile pepper
 Flaked coconut (optional)

1. Combine pineapple, papayas, and strawberries.
2. In a medium bowl combine lime juice, honey, cilantro, and ground ancho pepper. Drizzle over fruit. If desired, sprinkle with coconut and/or additional ancho chile. Serve immediately or cover and chill up to 4 hours. Makes 8 servings.
PER SERVING 117 cal., 1 g fat (0 g sat. fat), 0 mg chol., 8 mg sodium, 30 g carb., 4 g fiber, 1 g pro.

SPICED PUMPKIN COFFEE CREAMER

START TO FINISH 10 minutes

- 2 cups heavy cream or half-and-half
- 1 14-oz. can sweetened condensed milk
- 3 Tbsp. canned pumpkin
- 1 tsp. pumpkin pie spice
- 1 tsp. vanilla

1. In a 1-quart canning jar combine all the ingredients; seal. Store in refrigerator up to 2 weeks. Shake or stir before serving. Makes 56 servings.
PER SERVING 54 cal., 4 g fat (2 g sat. fat), 14 mg chol., 13 mg sodium, 4 g carb., 0 g fiber, 1 g pro.

Caramel Coffee Creamer Prepare as directed, except omit pumpkin and pumpkin pie spice. Substitute ¼ cup caramel-flavor ice cream topping.

BLOODY MARY MIX

START TO FINISH 10 minutes

- 1 46-oz. bottle hot-style or regular vegetable juice
- ½ cup freshly squeezed lemon juice
- 1 Tbsp. prepared horseradish
- 1 Tbsp. Worcestershire sauce
- 1 tsp. celery salt
 Ice cubes
 Vodka
 Black pepper (optional)
 Garnishes, such as sweet pickles, olives, cooked bacon strips, pepperoncini peppers, pickled green beans, and/or cooked shrimp (optional)

1. In a large pitcher combine the first five ingredients (through celery salt). Cover and chill until ready to serve.
2. For each drink, pour ½ cup mix into an ice-filled glass; add desired amount of vodka. If desired, sprinkle with pepper.
3. If desired, thread garnishes on long skewers. Add to each drink. Makes 12 servings.
PER SERVING 91 cal., 0 g fat, 0 mg chol., 366 mg sodium, 6 g carb., 1 g fiber, 1 g pro.

BLOODY MARY
MIX

SNICKERDOODLE
CIDER MIMOSA

SNICKERDOODLE CIDER MIMOSA

START TO FINISH 10 minutes

3   Tbsp. granulated sugar
1   tsp. ground cinnamon
2   cups apple cider
1   cup cream soda
4   cups sparkling white wine
    Apple slices (optional)

1. In a small shallow dish combine sugar and cinnamon. Moisten rims of eight rocks glasses with water. Dip rims of glasses into cinnamon-sugar.
2. Pour ¼ cup apple cider into each glass. Add 2 tablespoons cream soda to each glass. Top with ½ cup sparkling wine. Garnish with apple slices, if desired. Makes 8 servings.
PER SERVING *162 cal., 0 g fat, 0 mg chol., 16 mg sodium, 19 g carb., 0 g fiber, 0 g pro.*

MEXICAN HOT COFFEE COCKTAILS

START TO FINISH 15 minutes

6   cups prepared coffee
2   Tbsp. superfine or regular granulated
    sugar
¼   tsp. ground cinnamon
⅛   tsp. ground ancho chile pepper or
    cayenne pepper
    Chocolate-flavor syrup
¾   cup coffee liqueur, such as Kahlua
6   Tbsp. tequila, rum, or brandy
1   recipe Coffee Whipped Cream
12 chocolate-covered coffee beans,
    crushed

1. Pour coffee into a 2-quart insulated bottle to keep hot.
2. In a shallow dish stir together sugar, cinnamon, and ground ancho pepper. Wet rims of glass coffee mugs or brandy snifters with water then dip into sugar mixture.
3. For each cocktail, squeeze a little chocolate syrup in a design in a mug or glass. Add 2 tablespoons liqueur and 1 tablespoon tequila. Add 1 cup coffee. Top with Coffee Whipped Cream and coffee beans. Makes 6 servings.
Coffee Whipped Cream In a medium bowl combine ½ cup heavy cream, 1 teaspoon sugar, and ¼ teaspoon instant espresso coffee powder. Beat with a mixer on medium until soft peaks form.
PER SERVING *250 cal., 8 g fat (5 g sat. fat), 23 mg chol., 16 mg sodium, 25 g carb., 0 g fiber, 1 g pro.*

MEXICAN HOT COFFEE COCKTAILS

SPICED PUMPKIN
DINNER ROLLS,
PAGE 67

Tempting Breads

Enchant family and guests with extraordinary baked goods—traditional to culturally diverse—from this most enticing assortment of breads, buns, rolls,

MAPLE BUTTER TWISTS

MAPLE-BUTTER TWISTS

PREP 30 minutes
RISE 1 hour 45 minutes
REST 10 minutes
BAKE 25 minutes at 350°F

¼   cup warm water (105°F to 115°F)
1   packet active dry yeast
½   cup milk
¼   cup butter
3   Tbsp. granulated sugar
1½ tsp. salt
2   eggs
3¼ to 3½ cups all-purpose flour
½   cup packed brown sugar
⅓   cup granulated sugar
¼   cup butter, softened
¼   cup pure maple syrup
2   Tbsp. all-purpose flour
½   tsp. ground cinnamon
4   tsp. maple flavoring (optional)
½   cup chopped walnuts, toasted*
1   cup powdered sugar
3   to 4 tsp. water

1. In a large bowl combine warm water and yeast; set aside 5 minutes.
2. Meanwhile, in a small saucepan combine milk, ¼ cup butter, 3 tablespoons granulated sugar, and salt. Heat just until warm (120°F to 130°F) and butter is almost melted. Add to yeast mixture along with eggs.
3. Beat in as much of the flour as you can with a wooden spoon. Turn dough out onto a lightly floured surface. Knead in enough remaining flour to make a soft dough that is smooth and elastic. Shape dough into a ball. Place in a lightly greased bowl, turning once to grease surface of dough. Cover; let rise in a warm place until double in size, 1 to 1½ hours.
4. For filling, in a small bowl stir together the brown sugar, ⅓ cup granulated sugar, ¼ cup softened butter, maple syrup, 2 tablespoons flour, cinnamon, and maple flavoring (if using). Stir in walnuts. Lightly grease two 8-inch round baking pans; set aside.
5. Punch dough down. Divide in half. Cover; let rest 10 minutes. On a lightly floured surface, roll one portion of dough to a 14×8-inch rectangle. Spread half the filling. Starting from a long end, roll up dough and pinch edges to seal. Wrap ends together to form a ring. Place the ring, seam side down, in one prepared pan. Using a small

sharp knife, make eight cuts around the edge of dough at even intervals, cutting nearly through to center. Turn each cut portion so cut side faces up. Repeat with remaining dough and filling. Cover and let rise 45 minutes or until nearly double.

6. Meanwhile, preheat oven to 350°F. Bake rolls 25 to 30 minutes or until golden brown.

7. In a small bowl stir together powdered sugar and enough water to make a drizzling consistency. Drizzle over rolls. Serve warm or cooled. Makes 16 servings.

*Tip To toast nuts, preheat oven to 350°F. Spread nuts in a shallow baking pan. Bake 5 to 10 minutes or until light brown, shaking pan once or twice.

PER SERVING *279 cal., 9 g fat (4 g sat. fat), 42 mg chol., 274 mg sodium, 45 g carb., 1 g fiber, 5 g pro.*

JAM AND CREAM CHEESE ROLLS

PREP 30 minutes
RISE 3 hours 20 minutes
CHILL 6 hours
BAKE 15 minutes at 375°F

3½ cups all-purpose flour
½   cup warm water (105°F to 115°F)
1   pkg. active dry yeast
⅓   cup butter, softened
⅓   cup sugar
¾   tsp. salt
4   eggs
1   8-oz. pkg. cream cheese, softened
3   Tbsp. sugar
     Dash salt
½   cup seedless raspberry jam, orange marmalade, or other jam or preserves
½   tsp. ground cinnamon

1. In a small bowl stir together ¼ cup of the flour, the water, and yeast. Let stand 20 minutes or until mixture starts to bubble.

2. In a large bowl beat butter, ⅓ cup sugar, and ¾ teaspoon salt with a mixer on low to medium until fluffy. Beat in 1 cup of the flour. Add three of the eggs; beat on high 3 minutes. Beat in yeast mixture. Stir in remaining 2¼ cups flour until smooth. Transfer to a greased bowl. Cover and let rise in a warm place until double in size (about 2 hours). Chill dough 6 hours.

JAM AND CREAM CHEESE ROLLS

3. Let dough stand at room temperature 30 minutes. Meanwhile, in a medium bowl beat cream cheese, 2 tablespoons of the sugar, and dash salt with a mixer on medium 3 minutes or until smooth.

4. On a lightly floured surface, roll dough into a 12-inch square. Cut into nine 4-inch squares. Spoon 1½ tablespoons cream cheese mixture onto each square; top with 2 teaspoons jam. Bring edges of dough up over filling and pinch together to seal.

5. Place rolls, seam sides down, 2 inches apart on a greased large baking sheet. Cover and let rise in a warm place until nearly double in size (about 30 minutes).

6. Preheat oven to 375°F. In a small bowl combine remaining 1 tablespoon sugar and the cinnamon. Beat remaining egg with a fork then brush lightly over rolls. Sprinkle with cinnamon-sugar. Bake 15 to 18 minutes or until golden. Transfer to a wire rack to cool. Makes 9 servings.

PER SERVING *455 cal., 18 g fat (10 g sat. fat), 126 mg chol., 383 mg sodium, 63 g carb., 2 g fiber, 10 g pro.*

To Store Freeze cooled rolls in a labeled freezer bag or container up to 3 months. Thaw at room temperature.

ORANGE-SPICE CHALLAH BUNS

TWO-TONE BALSAMIC-ONION SPIRAL ROLLS

PREP 35 minutes
COOL 15 minutes
RISE 45 minutes
BAKE 25 minutes at 375°F

2	slices bacon
2	cups chopped onions
¼	cup balsamic vinegar
½	cup grated Parmesan cheese
¼	tsp. black pepper
1	1-lb. loaf frozen white bread dough, thawed
1	1-lb. loaf frozen whole wheat bread dough, thawed
1	egg yolk, lightly beaten
1	Tbsp. milk
	Creamy stone-ground mustard (optional)

1. Grease a 13×9-inch baking pan; set aside. In a large skillet cook bacon until crisp. Using a slotted spoon, transfer bacon to paper towels, reserving drippings in skillet. Crumble bacon and set aside. Add onions to skillet; cook on medium heat 5 minutes or until tender. Carefully stir in balsamic vinegar. Simmer, uncovered, over medium-low heat 1 to 2 minutes or until most of the liquid has evaporated. Remove from heat. Stir in Parmesan cheese and pepper. Cool completely.

2. Meanwhile, on a lightly floured surface, roll each bread dough into a 10×16-inch rectangle. Spread onion mixture on white dough; sprinkle with bacon. Top with whole wheat dough. Starting from a long side, roll up rectangles together. Seal seam. Slice roll crosswise into 16 pieces. Place pieces, cut sides down, in pan.

3. Cover loosely and let rise in a warm place until nearly double in size (about 45 minutes). Meanwhile, preheat oven to 375°F. In a small bowl beat together egg yolk and milk; brush over rolls.

4. Bake, uncovered, 25 minutes or until roll tops are golden brown. Invert rolls onto a wire rack. Cool 15 minutes. Invert onto a serving platter. Serve warm, if desired, with creamy stone-ground mustard. Makes 16 servings.

PER SERVING *189 cal., 4 g fat (1 g sat. fat), 18 mg chol., 237 mg sodium, 29 g carb., 1 g fiber, 7 g pro.*

ORANGE-SPICE CHALLAH BUNS

PREP 35 minutes
RISE 2 hours 30 minutes
BAKE 18 minutes at 350°F
COOL 15 minutes

1	pkg. active dry yeast (2¼ tsp.)
1	cup warm water
2	tsp. orange zest
½	cup orange juice
6	cups all-purpose flour, plus more for dusting
¼	cup sugar
2	tsp. ground cinnamon
1½	tsp. kosher salt
½	tsp. cardamom
⅔	cup canola or vegetable oil
2	large eggs
1	egg
1	Tbsp. water
	Pearl decorating sugar or coarse decorating sugar

1. In a medium bowl combine the yeast, warm water, and orange juice. Let stand 5 minutes or until slightly foamy. Meanwhile, in a large bowl or bowl of stand mixer combine the flour, sugar, orange zest, cinnamon, salt, and cardamom. In a medium bowl whisk together oil and 2 eggs. Add yeast mixture and egg mixture to flour mixture; stir to combine.

2. Knead dough (by hand on floured surface or with dough hooks on medium 7 to 10 minutes), adding a little flour if necessary for a smooth and slightly sticky dough.

3. Transfer dough to an extra-large greased bowl. Cover with plastic wrap and let stand at room temperature until double in size (about 2 hours). (Alternatively, chill dough in refrigerator overnight, then let stand at room temperature 1 hour before shaping.)

4. Punch dough down. Turn out onto a lightly floured surface. Divide dough into 18 pieces; shape into balls. Place on 2 baking sheets lined with parchment paper. Loosely cover and let rise 30 minutes.

5. Preheat oven to 350°F. In a small bowl whisk together egg and 1 tablespoon water. Brush buns with egg wash; sprinkle with pearl sugar. Bake 18 to 20 minutes or until golden brown (internal temperature 190°F). Slide buns onto wire racks; cool at least 15 minutes before serving. Makes 18 servings.

PER SERVING *257 cal., 9 g fat (1 g sat. fat), 31 mg chol., 107 mg sodium, 37 g carb., 1 g fiber, 6 g pro.*

TWO-TONE
BALSAMIC-ONION
SPIRAL ROLLS

CHALLAH

CHALLAH

PREP 35 minutes
RISE 2 hours 30 minutes
BAKE 30 minutes at 375°F
COOL 30 minutes

1½ cups warm water (105°F to 115°F)
2 pkg. active dry yeast (about 4½ tsp.)
½ cup plus 1 tsp. sugar
6½ cups all-purpose flour, plus more for dusting
2 tsp. kosher salt
4 eggs
⅔ cup canola or vegetable oil
1 egg yolk
1 Tbsp. water
½ tsp. sea salt flakes

1. In a small bowl stir together the 1½ cups warm water, yeast, and 1 teaspoon sugar. Let stand 5 minutes or until slightly foamy. Meanwhile, in a large bowl or bowl of stand mixer mix together flour, kosher salt, and ¼ cup of the sugar. In a medium bowl whisk together four eggs, oil, and remaining ¼ cup sugar. Add yeast mixture and egg mixture to flour mixture; stir.
2. Knead (by hand on floured surface or with dough hook on medium 7 to 10 minutes), adding a small amount of flour if necessary, for a smooth and slightly sticky dough. Shape dough into a ball. Place in an extra-large lightly greased bowl. Cover with plastic wrap; let rise until nearly double in size (2 hours). (Or chill dough in refrigerator overnight; let stand at room temperature 1 hour before shaping.)
3. Punch dough down. Turn out onto a lightly floured surface. Divide dough into four* portions. Roll each portion into a rope about 3 feet long. Shape ropes into spirals. Place loaves at least 3 inches apart on two large baking sheets lined with parchment paper. Cover loosely; let rise 30 minutes.
4. Preheat oven to 375°F. In a small bowl whisk together egg yolk and 1 tablespoon water. Brush the loaves with a thin, even layer of egg wash; sprinkle with sea salt. Bake 30 minutes or until loaves are golden brown (internal temperature 190°F). Transfer loaves to wire racks to cool at least 30 minutes before slicing. Makes 24 servings.
*Tip To make two loaves, halve all ingredients and shape into two loaves.

PER SERVING *212 cal., 7 g fat (1 g sat. fat), 39 mg chol., 155 mg sodium, 31 g carb., 1 g fiber, 5 g pro.*
Whole Wheat Challah Substitute up to 2½ cups whole wheat flour for an equal amount of all-purpose flour (this dough may take slightly longer to rise).

CINNAMON-STREUSEL BABKA

PREP 40 minutes
RISE 2 hours 15 minutes
REST 10 minutes
BAKE 1 hour 10 minutes at 325°F

3 cups all-purpose flour
1 pkg. active dry yeast
¾ cup milk
½ cup butter, cut up
¼ cup sugar
1 tsp. salt
1 egg
⅓ cup sugar
1 Tbsp. ground cinnamon
3 Tbsp. butter, melted
1 egg
1 Tbsp. heavy cream
1 Tbsp. packed brown sugar
¼ tsp. ground cinnamon
⅛ tsp. salt
3 Tbsp. all-purpose flour

1. In a large bowl stir together 2 cups of the flour and the yeast; set aside. In a small saucepan heat and stir milk, ½ cup butter, ¼ cup sugar, and salt until warm (120°F to 130°F) and butter is almost melted. Add to flour mixture along with one egg. Stir with a sturdy spoon until combined. Stir in as much remaining flour as you can.
2. Turn dough out onto a lightly floured surface. Knead in remaining flour to make a soft dough that is smooth and elastic (about 3 minutes). Shape dough into a ball. Place in a lightly greased bowl; turn once to grease surface of dough. Cover; let rise in a warm place until nearly double in size (1½ to 2 hours).
3. Punch dough down. Turn out onto a lightly floured surface. Cover and let rest 10 minutes. Grease an 8×4-inch loaf pan. For filling, in a small bowl combine ⅓ cup sugar and 1 tablespoon cinnamon. Roll dough into a 16×12-inch rectangle. Brush with 2 tablespoons melted butter and sprinkle with cinnamon-sugar. Roll up rectangle, starting from a long side. Cut roll in half crosswise. Arrange pieces

in an X. Twist each end together. Place dough twist in prepared pan. Cover and let rise in a warm place until nearly double (45 to 60 minutes).
4. Preheat oven to 325°F. Whisk together one egg and the cream. Brush over loaf. For streusel, in a small bowl stir together the brown sugar, ¼ teaspoon cinnamon, and ⅛ teaspoon salt. Stir in 1 remaining tablespoon melted butter. Add 3 tablespoons flour and toss until small clumps form. Sprinkle streusel over loaf.
5. Bake 70 to 75 minutes or until golden and bread sounds hollow when gently tapped (internal temperature 180°F to 190°F), covering with foil the last 20 to 25 minutes to prevent overbrowning. Loosen loaf from pan and transfer to a wire rack to cool completely. Makes 12 servings.
Babka Braids Prepare as above, except after cutting dough roll in half crosswise, cut each piece lengthwise into thirds (some filling will fall out). For each loaf, braid three pieces together and sprinkle with filling that falls out. Place each braid on a parchment paper-lined baking sheet. Let rise; bake 45 minutes.
PER SERVING *284 cal., 12 g fat (7 g sat. fat), 62 mg chol., 323 mg sodium, 38 g carb., 1 g fiber, 5 g pro.*

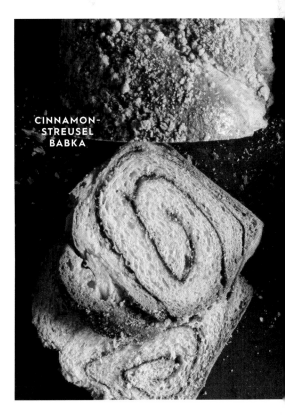

CINNAMON-STREUSEL BABKA

SPICED PUMPKIN DINNER ROLLS

SPICED PUMPKIN DINNER ROLLS

PREP 30 minutes
RISE 1 hour 30 minutes
REST 10 minutes
BAKE 20 minutes at 400°F

4½ to 5 cups all-purpose flour
1   pkg. active dry yeast
1   cup warm milk (120°F to 130°F)
1   cup canned pumpkin
⅓   cup butter, melted
¼   cup packed brown sugar
1¼ tsp. salt
1   tsp. ground cinnamon
1   tsp. ground coriander
¼   to ½ tsp. cayenne pepper
2   Tbsp. butter, melted
    Black and/or white sesame seeds

1. In a large bowl combine 2 cups of the flour and the yeast. In another bowl combine the next eight ingredients (through cayenne). Add pumpkin mixture to flour mixture. Beat with a mixer on low 30 seconds, scraping bowl as needed. Beat on high 3 minutes. Stir in as much remaining flour as you can.
2. Turn dough out onto a lightly floured surface. Knead in enough remaining flour to make a moderately soft dough that is smooth and elastic (3 to 5 minutes

total). Place dough in a greased bowl, turn once to grease surface of dough. Cover; let rise in a warm place until double in size (1 to 1½ hours).
3. Punch dough down. Turn out onto a lightly floured surface. Cover; let rest 10 minutes. Meanwhile, grease a 13×9-inch baking pan. With lightly floured hands divide dough into 15 pieces; shape into balls. Arrange balls in prepared pan. Cover; let rise in a warm place until nearly double in size (30 to 40 minutes).
4. Preheat oven to 400°F. Brush tops with the 2 tablespoons melted butter. Sprinkle with sesame seeds. Bake 20 to 25 minutes or until rolls are golden and sound hollow when lightly tapped. Remove rolls from pan; serve warm. Makes 15 servings.
PER SERVING *217 cal., 6 g fat (4 g sat. fat), 16 mg chol., 249 mg sodium, 35 g carb., 2 g fiber, 5 g pro.*

BUTTERMILK-SAGE DINNER ROLLS

PREP 45 minutes
RISE 1 hour
BAKE 15 minutes at 375°F

8   Tbsp. (1 stick) butter, cut up
10 fresh sage leaves, chopped

3   Tbsp. sugar
1½ cups buttermilk
2   pkg. active dry yeast
½   cup warm water (105°F to 115°F)
4½ cups all-purpose flour
2   tsp. kosher salt
½   tsp. baking soda
½   tsp. dried sage, crushed (optional)
2   Tbsp. unsalted butter, melted

1. Lightly grease twenty-four 2½-inch muffin cups. In a medium saucepan combine butter, sage, and 2 tablespoons of the sugar. Heat and stir over medium-high heat just until butter is melted. Stir in buttermilk and heat just until warmed (do not boil). Remove from heat; cool to room temperature.
2. In a small bowl combine the yeast and remaining 1 tablespoon sugar. Stir in the warm water; let stand about 5 minutes or until yeast foams. Add yeast mixture to buttermilk mixture; stir to combine.
3. In a large bowl stir together the flour, salt, and baking soda. Add buttermilk-yeast mixture. Stir to form a sticky dough. Loosely cover bowl; let stand in a warm place or until dough has risen slightly (about 30 minutes).
4. Preheat oven to 375°F. Turn dough out onto a lightly floured surface. Knead several times or until dough is easy to handle. Pinch off pieces of dough and form into 1-inch balls. To shape cloverleaf rolls, place three 1-inch balls in each prepared muffin cup. Loosely cover rolls with a clean cloth and let rise in a warm place until double in size (30 to 45 minutes).
5. If desired, stir dried sage into the melted butter. Uncover rolls. Brush lightly with melted butter. Bake 15 minutes or until golden brown. Remove rolls from muffin cups. Serve warm. Makes 24 servings.
PER SERVING *142 cal., 5 g fat (3 g sat. fat), 13 mg chol., 205 mg sodium, 20 g carb., 1 g fiber, 3 g pro.*
Make Ahead Prepare dough as directed through Step 4. Transfer dough to an airtight container; cover. Store in refrigerator up to 24 hours. Remove from refrigerator and let stand at room temperature 20 minutes. Continue as directed.

BUTTERMILK-SAGE
DINNER ROLLS

VEGGIE
QUICK
BREAD

VEGGIE QUICK BREAD

PREP 25 minutes
BAKE 55 minutes at 350°F
COOL 10 minutes

1   cup all-purpose flour
½   cup whole wheat pastry flour or
      whole wheat flour
1½ tsp. baking powder
¾   tsp. ground cinnamon
½   tsp. salt
1   egg, lightly beaten
¾   cup sugar
⅔   cup finely shredded zucchini
½   cup canola or vegetable oil
⅓   cup finely shredded peeled carrot
⅓   cup finely shredded peeled
      rutabaga
¼   cup honey
1   tsp. vanilla
½   cup chopped pecans or walnuts

1. Preheat oven to 350°F. Grease the
bottom and ½ inch up the sides of an
8×4×2-inch loaf pan; set aside. In a large
bowl stir together all-purpose flour, whole
wheat flour, baking powder, cinnamon,
and salt. Make a well in center.
2. In a medium bowl combine egg,
sugar, zucchini, oil, carrot, rutabaga,
honey, and vanilla. Add zucchini mixture
all at once to flour mixture; stir just
until moistened (batter will be lumpy).
Spoon batter into prepared loaf pan,
spreading evenly. Sprinkle with nuts.
3. Bake 55 to 60 minutes or until a
toothpick inserted near center comes
out clean. Cool in pan on a wire rack
10 minutes. Remove bread from pan.
Cool completely on wire rack. Wrap and
store overnight before slicing. Makes
12 servings.
PER SERVING *249 cal., 13 g fat (1 g sat.
fat), 16 mg chol., 168 mg sodium, 32 g
carb., 2 g fiber, 3 g pro.*

BROWNED BUTTER SAGE CORNMEAL MUFFINS

PREP 20 minutes
COOK 15 minutes
BAKE 20 minutes at 350°F
COOL 5 minutes

6   Tbsp. butter
1¼ cups coarsely ground cornmeal
1   cup all-purpose flour
1   Tbsp. sugar
1½ tsp. baking powder

**BROWNED BUTTER
SAGE CORNMEAL
MUFFINS**

½   tsp. salt
¼   tsp. baking soda
1   egg, lightly beaten
1¼ cups buttermilk
12   to 24 small fresh sage leaves
1   tsp. olive or canola oil

1. Preheat oven to 350°F. Grease twelve
2½-inch muffin cups; set aside.
2. For browned butter, in a small heavy
saucepan cook butter over medium
heat 15 minutes or until lightly browned.
Pour browned butter into a small
heatproof bowl; cool slightly.
3. Meanwhile, in a large bowl whisk
together the next six ingredients

(through baking soda). Make a well in
center of flour mixture; set aside. In a
medium bowl whisk together cooled
browned butter, egg, and buttermilk.
Add buttermilk mixture to flour mixture,
stirring to combine. Spoon batter into
muffin cups, filling each three-fourths full.
Lightly brush both sides of sage leaves
with oil; place on batter in muffin cups.
4. Bake 20 minutes or until lightly
browned. Cool in muffin cups 5 minutes.
Transfer muffins to a wire rack to cool
slightly. Serve warm. Makes 12 servings.
PER SERVING *167 cal., 7 g fat (4 g sat.
fat), 32 mg chol., 263 mg sodium, 22 g
carb., 1 g fiber, 4 g pro.*

CRANBERRY SCONES

PREP 25 minutes
BAKE 12 minutes at 400°F

1   cup fresh or frozen cranberries
2½ cups all-purpose flour
⅔   cup sugar
2½ tsp. baking powder
½   tsp. baking soda
¾   cup cold butter, sliced
¾   cup buttermilk
1   recipe Frosting

1. Preheat oven to 400°F. Rinse cranberries in cold water; drain. Slice or coarsely chop cranberries; set aside. Lightly grease two baking sheets or line with parchment paper; set aside.
2. In a large bowl combine flour, sugar, baking powder, and baking soda. Using a pastry blender, cut in cold butter until mixture resembles coarse crumbs. Make a well in center of flour mixture; set aside.
3. In a medium bowl combine buttermilk and cranberries. Add buttermilk mixture all at once to flour mixture. Stir just until combined.
4. Turn dough out onto a lightly floured surface. Knead dough by folding and gently pressing 10 to 12 strokes or until dough is nearly smooth. Divide dough in half. Pat or lightly roll each dough half into an 8-inch circle. Cut each into eight wedges. Place dough wedges 2 inches apart on prepared baking sheets.
5. Bake 12 to 14 minutes or until scones are golden brown. Transfer scones to wire racks to cool slightly. Spread tops with frosting. Serve warm. Makes 16 servings.
Frosting In a medium bowl beat 1 tablespoons butter and ½ teaspoon almond extract with a mixer on medium 30 seconds. Gradually add 1½ cups powdered sugar and 2 tablespoons milk, beating until well combined. Spread frosting on slightly cooled scones.
PER SERVING *239 cal., 10 g fat (6 g sat. fat), 25 mg chol., 157 mg sodium, 36 g carb., 1 g fiber, 3 g pro.*

CRANBERRY SCONES

BLUEBERRY
BANANA BREAD

BLUEBERRY BANANA BREAD

PREP 25 minutes
BAKE 50 minutes at 350°F
COOL 10 minutes

2	cups all-purpose flour
1½	tsp. baking powder
1	tsp. ground cinnamon
½	tsp. baking soda
¼	tsp. salt
¼	tsp. ground ginger
¼	tsp. ground nutmeg
2	eggs, lightly beaten
1	cup granulated sugar
½	cup vegetable oil or melted butter
1½	cups mashed ripe bananas*
¾	cup fresh or frozen blueberries
1	Tbsp. all-purpose flour
¼	cup chopped walnuts
¼	cup flaked coconut
1	recipe Streusel-Nut Topping

1. Preheat oven to 350°F. Grease bottom and ½ inch up sides of one 9×5-inch loaf pan. In a large bowl stir together first seven ingredients (through nutmeg). Make a well in center of flour mixture.
2. In a medium bowl combine eggs, granulated sugar, and oil; stir in mashed bananas. Add banana mixture all at once to flour mixture. Stir just until moistened (batter should be lumpy). In a small bowl toss together blueberries and 1 tablespoon flour. Fold blueberries, walnuts, and coconut into batter. Spoon batter into prepared loaf pan. Sprinkle with Streusel Nut Topping.
3. Bake 50 to 55 minutes or until a toothpick inserted near center comes out clean (to prevent overbrowning, cover loosely with foil the last 15 minutes). Cool in pan on a wire rack 10 minutes. Remove from pan; cool on wire rack. Wrap and store overnight before slicing. Makes 16 servings.
Streusel-Nut Topping In a small bowl stir together 3 tablespoons packed brown sugar and 2 tablespoons all-purpose flour. Using a pastry blender, cut in 4 teaspoons butter until mixture resembles coarse crumbs. Stir in ¼ cup chopped walnuts.
*Roasted Bananas For exceptionally deep banana flavor, roast three medium bananas. Line a 15×10-inch baking pan with foil. Arrange unpeeled bananas in prepared pan. Prick banana skins with a fork at 1-inch intervals. Bake 15 minutes;

EGGNOG MUFFINS

cool bananas in pan. Using a small sharp knife, split banana peels. Measure 1½ cups roasted bananas, pressing gently into measuring cups.
PER SERVING 220 cal., 9 g fat (1 g sat. fat), 23 mg chol., 131 mg sodium, 34 g carb., 2 g fiber, 3 g pro.

EGGNOG MUFFINS

PREP 25 minutes
BAKE 18 minutes at 375°F
COOL 5 minutes

2¼	cups all-purpose flour
1	cup sugar
2	tsp. baking powder
½	tsp. ground nutmeg
2	eggs, lightly beaten
1	cup eggnog
½	cup butter, melted and cooled
1	tsp. vanilla
½	tsp. rum extract
1	recipe Nutmeg-Streusel Topping

1. Preheat oven to 375°F. Grease twelve 2½-inch muffin cups or line with paper bake cups; set aside. In a medium bowl combine flour, sugar, baking powder, and nutmeg. Make a well in center of flour mixture; set aside.
2. In another bowl combine eggs, eggnog, butter, vanilla, and rum extract. Add egg mixture all at once to flour mixture. Stir just until moistened (batter should be lumpy). Spoon batter into prepared muffin cups, filling each two-thirds full. Sprinkle Nutmeg-Streusel Topping over muffin batter in cups.
3. Bake 18 to 20 minutes or until golden and a toothpick inserted into centers comes out clean. Cool in muffin cups on a wire rack 5 minutes. Remove from muffin cups; serve warm. Makes 12 servings.
Nutmeg-Streusel Topping In a small bowl stir together ⅓ cup all-purpose flour, ⅓ cup sugar, and ½ teaspoon nutmeg. Using a pastry blender, cut in 2 tablespoons butter until mixture resembles coarse crumbs.
PER SERVING 312 cal., 12 g fat (7 g sat. fat), 73 mg chol., 132 mg sodium, 46 g carb., 1 g fiber, 5 g pro.

APPLE COFFEE CAKE

PREP 35 minutes
BAKE 40 minutes at 350°F

1½ to 2 cups chopped, peeled apples
¼ cup water
1¼ cups sugar
2 Tbsp. cornstarch
1½ cups all-purpose flour
½ tsp. baking powder
¼ tsp. baking soda
¼ cup butter
1 egg, lightly beaten
½ cup buttermilk or sour milk*
½ tsp. vanilla
¼ cup all-purpose flour
2 Tbsp. butter

1. For filling, in a medium saucepan combine apples and water. Bring to boiling; reduce heat. Simmer, covered, about 5 minutes or until apples are tender. Combine ¼ cup of the sugar and the cornstarch; stir into apples. Cook and stir over medium heat until thickened and bubbly. Cook and stir 2 minutes more; remove from heat.

2. Preheat oven to 350°F. In a medium bowl combine the 1½ cups flour, ¾ cup of the sugar, baking powder, and baking soda. Cut in ¼ cup butter until mixture resembles coarse crumbs. Make a well in center of flour mixture.

3. In another bowl combine egg, buttermilk, and vanilla. Add egg mixture all at once to flour mixture. Stir just until moistened (batter should be lumpy). Spread half the batter into an ungreased 8-inch-square baking pan. Gently spread filling over batter. Drop remaining batter in small mounds onto filling.

4. In a bowl stir together the ¼ cup flour and remaining ¼ cup sugar. Cut in 2 tablespoons butter until mixture resembles coarse crumbs. Sprinkle on coffee cake. Bake 40 to 45 minutes or until golden. Serve warm. Makes 9 servings.

*Tip For ½ cup milk, place 1½ teaspoons lemon juice or vinegar in a glass measuring cup. Add milk to equal ½ cup. Let stand 5 minutes before using.

PER SERVING *298 cal., 9 g fat (5 g sat. fat), 44 mg chol., 126 mg sodium, 52 g carb., 1 g fiber, 4 g pro.*

COCONUT-PECAN COFFEE CAKE

PREP 30 minutes
BAKE 55 minutes at 325°F
COOL 1 hour

½ cup butter, softened
1 cup sugar
2 tsp. baking powder
½ tsp. baking soda
¼ tsp. salt
2 eggs
1 tsp. vanilla
2¼ cups all-purpose flour
1 8-oz. carton sour cream
1 recipe Coconut-Pecan Topping
    Powdered sugar and unsweetened cocoa powder (optional)

1. Preheat oven to 325°F. Grease and flour a 10-inch fluted tube pan; set aside. In a large bowl beat butter on medium 30 seconds. Add the sugar, baking powder, baking soda, and salt. Beat until well combined, scraping sides of bowl occasionally. Add eggs, one at a time, beating well after each addition. Beat in vanilla. Alternately add flour and sour cream, beating on low after each addition just until combined.

2. Sprinkle half the Coconut-Pecan Topping in prepared pan. Spoon half the batter in mounds over topping; carefully spread evenly. Sprinkle with remaining topping. Spoon on remaining batter, spreading evenly.

3. Bake 55 to 65 minutes or until a wooden toothpick inserted near center comes out clean. Cool in pan on a wire rack 10 minutes. Remove cake from pan; cool completely on wire rack. If desired, dust cake with a mixture of powdered sugar and cocoa powder. Makes 12 servings.

Coconut-Pecan Topping In a large bowl combine 1 cup all-purpose flour, 1 cup packed brown sugar, and 1 teaspoon ground cinnamon. Using a pastry blender, cut in ½ cup cold butter, cut up, until mixture resembles coarse crumbs. Stir in ¾ cup semisweet chocolate pieces, ½ cup flaked coconut, and ½ cup chopped pecans.

PER SERVING *550 cal., 28 g fat (16 g sat. fat), 86 mg chol., 297 mg sodium, 71 g carb., 2 g fiber, 6 g pro.*

APPLE COFFEE CAKE

COCONUT-PECAN
COFFEE CAKE

Just Desserts

Take your pick from fabulous pies, tarts, cheesecakes, and over-the-top cakes—all superb endings to festive holiday occasions.

MEYER LEMON POTS DE CREME, PAGE 93

BITTERSWEET
CHOCOLATE TART,
PAGE 88

CRANBERRY-ORANGE UPSIDE-DOWN SPICE CAKE

PREP 20 minutes
BAKE 35 minutes at 350°F
COOL 3 minutes

1½ cups all-purpose flour
1 tsp. baking powder
½ tsp. ground ginger
½ tsp. ground cinnamon
¼ tsp. baking soda
¼ tsp. salt
3 Tbsp. butter
¾ cup packed brown sugar
1 11-oz. can mandarin orange sections, drained
1 cup fresh or frozen cranberries
2 eggs, lightly beaten
¾ cup plain Greek yogurt or sour cream
¾ cup granulated sugar
6 Tbsp. butter, melted
1 tsp. vanilla

1. Preheat oven to 350°F. In a large bowl stir together the first six ingredients (through salt). Set aside. Add the 3 tablespoons butter to a 10×2-inch cast-iron or other heavy oven-going skillet. Place skillet in oven 3 to 5 minutes, just until butter is melted. Carefully remove from oven and tip skillet to coat sides with butter.
2. Sprinkle brown sugar on bottom of skillet. Arrange orange sections on brown sugar. Top with cranberries.
3. In a bowl combine the last five ingredients. One-third at a time, add flour mixture to egg mixture, stirring just until combined after each addition. Spoon batter into skillet, spreading to cover fruit.
4. Bake 35 to 40 minutes or until a wooden toothpick inserted in center comes out clean. Cool in skillet on a wire rack 3 to 4 minutes. Run a knife around edges of cake to loosen. Invert cake onto a platter. Replace any fruit that remains in skillet. Serve warm or at room temperature. Makes 8 servings.
PER SERVING *408 cal., 15 g fat (9 g sat. fat), 84 mg chol., 320 mg sodium, 63 g carb., 2 g fiber, 6 g pro.*

BANANA-COCONUT COFFEE CAKE WITH MACADAMIA NUT STREUSEL

PREP 30 minutes
BAKE 35 minutes at 350°F
COOL 30 minutes

3½ cups all-purpose flour
¾ cup flaked coconut
1 Tbsp. baking powder
1 tsp. baking soda
1 tsp. salt
1 cup butter, softened
¾ cup granulated sugar
¾ cup packed brown sugar
4 eggs
3 ripe bananas, mashed
¼ cup coffee liqueur or strong brewed coffee
¼ cup milk
2 tsp. vanilla
¼ cup all-purpose flour
¼ cup packed brown sugar
½ tsp. ground cinnamon
¼ cup butter, cut up
½ cup coarsely chopped macadamia nuts
1 recipe Powdered Sugar Icing

1. Preheat oven to 350°F. Grease and flour a 13×9-inch baking pan. In a bowl stir together the first five ingredients (through salt).
2. In an extra-large bowl beat the 1 cup butter, ¾ cup granulated sugar, and ¾ cup brown sugar with a mixer on medium to high until light and fluffy. Scrape sides of bowl; beat 1 minute. Add eggs, one at a time, beating well after each addition. Beat in bananas, liqueur, milk, and vanilla on low just until combined (mixture may appear curdled). Add flour mixture, beating on low just until combined. Spread batter into prepared pan.
3. For streusel, in a bowl stir together the ¼ cup flour, ¼ cup brown sugar, and cinnamon. Using a pastry blender, cut in the ¼ cup butter until mixture resembles coarse crumbs. Stir in macadamia nuts. Sprinkle evenly over batter.
4. Bake 35 to 40 minutes or until a toothpick inserted near center comes out clean. Cool in pan on wire rack 30 minutes. Drizzle with Powdered Sugar Icing. Serve warm. Makes 18 servings.
Powdered Sugar Icing In a bowl stir together ¾ cup powdered sugar, 4 teaspoons milk, ½ teaspoon vanilla, and, if desired, a few drops coconut extract until smooth.
PER SERVING *364 cal., 18 g fat (10 g sat. fat), 76 mg chol., 424 mg sodium, 45 g carb., 2 g fiber, 5 g pro.*

CRANBERRY-ORANGE UPSIDE-DOWN SPICE CAKE

CHOCOLATE TIRAMISU CAKE ROLL

PREP 40 minutes
BAKE 15 minutes at 375°F
COOL 1 hour
CHILL 2 hours

- ⅓ cup all-purpose flour
- ¼ cup unsweetened cocoa powder
- 1 oz. dark chocolate, grated
- ¼ tsp. baking soda
- ¼ tsp. salt
- 4 eggs, room temperature
- 1 Tbsp. instant espresso coffee powder
- 1 cup sugar
- ¼ cup water
- 1 Tbsp. coffee liqueur or cooled strong coffee
- 1 recipe Cream Cheese Filling
- 1½ oz. dark chocolate, melted (optional)

1. Preheat oven to 375°F. Grease a 15×10-inch baking pan. Line bottom with parchment paper; grease and lightly flour parchment. In a small bowl stir together the first five ingredients (through salt).

2. In a large bowl beat eggs and espresso powder with a mixer on high 5 minutes. Gradually add ¾ cup of the sugar, beating 5 minutes more or until thick. Fold in flour mixture. Spread batter into prepared pan.

3. Bake 15 minutes or until top springs back when lightly touched. Immediately loosen edges of cake from pan and turn cake out onto a towel sprinkled with additional cocoa powder. Carefully peel off parchment. Starting from a short side, roll towel and cake into a spiral. Cool on a wire rack 1 hour.

4. For syrup, in a small saucepan combine remaining ¼ cup sugar and the water. Bring to boiling over medium heat, stirring to dissolve sugar. Remove from heat. Stir in liqueur; cool.

5. Unroll cake; remove towel. Brush cake with syrup. Spread with Cream Cheese Filling to within 1 inch of edges. Roll up cake; trim ends. Cover and chill 2 to 24 hours. If desired, drizzle with melted chocolate. Makes 12 servings.

Cream Cheese Filling In a medium bowl beat 4 ounces softened, light cream cheese spread with a mixer on medium until smooth. Gradually beat in 2 tablespoons fat-free milk. Beat in 2 tablespoons unsweetened cocoa powder and 1½ tablespoons coffee liqueur or cooled strong coffee. Fold in 1 cup frozen light whipped dessert topping, thawed.

PER SERVING *171 cal., 6 g fat (3 g sat. fat), 69 mg chol., 148 mg sodium, 27 g carb., 1 g fiber, 4 g pro.*

**CHOCOLATE
TIRAMISU
CAKE ROLL**

HUMMINGBIRD CAKE

PREP 30 minutes
BAKE 30 minutes at 350°F
COOL 10 minutes

- 1 pkg. 2-layer-size spice cake mix
- 1 8-oz. can crushed pineapple, undrained
- 1 very ripe banana, mashed (⅓ cup)
- ½ cup vegetable oil
- ½ cup water
- 2 eggs, lightly beaten
- 1 8-oz. pkg. cream cheese, softened
- ½ cup butter, softened
- 2 tsp. vanilla
- 5½ to 6 cups powdered sugar
  Chopped pecans, toasted (tip, page 34)

HUMMINGBIRD CAKE

1. Preheat oven to 350°F. Grease and flour two 8-inch-round cake pans; set aside. In a large bowl combine the first six ingredients (through eggs). Beat with a mixer on low just until combined. Increase to medium and beat 2 minutes more. Spoon batter into prepared pans. Bake 30 to 35 minutes or until a toothpick inserted near centers comes out clean.

2. Cool cakes in pans on a wire rack 10 minutes. Remove from pans and cool completely on wire racks.

3. For frosting, in a large bowl beat cream cheese, butter, and vanilla with a mixer on medium until light and fluffy. Gradually beat in powdered sugar to reach spreading consistency.

4. To assemble, place one cake layer, bottom side up, on a serving platter.

Spread with ¾ cup frosting. Top with second layer, bottom side up. Spread top and sides of cake with remaining frosting. Sprinkle top of cake with chopped pecans. Makes 12 servings.
PER SERVING 663 cal., 30 g fat (11 g sat. fat), 72 mg chol., 422 mg sodium, 96 g carb., 1 g fiber, 5 g pro.

COCONUT LAYER CAKE

PREP 45 minutes
BAKE 25 minutes at 350°F
COOL 2 hours

4   eggs
2   cups all-purpose flour
1½ tsp. baking powder
¼   tsp. salt
2   cups sugar
1   cup milk
¼   cup butter
1½ tsp. vanilla
1   recipe Coconut Filling
1   recipe Crème Fraîche Frosting
     Fresh coconut curls or
     unsweetened large coconut flakes,
     toasted*

1. Allow eggs to stand at room temperature 30 minutes. Meanwhile, grease and lightly flour two 9×1½-inch or 8×1½-inch round cake pans; set pans aside. In a medium bowl stir together flour, baking powder, and salt; set aside.
2. Preheat oven to 350°F. In a large bowl beat eggs with a mixer on high 4 minutes or until thickened. Gradually beat in sugar on medium until light and fluffy (4 to 5 minutes). Add the flour mixture; beat on low just until combined (mixture will be thick).
3. In a small saucepan heat and stir milk and butter over low heat until butter is melted; stir in vanilla. Add to batter; beat until combined (batter will be thin). Pour batter into prepared pans; spread evenly.
4. Bake 25 to 30 minutes or until a wooden toothpick inserted in centers comes out clean. Cool cake layers in pans on wire racks 10 minutes. Remove layers from pans; cool thoroughly on wire racks.
5. Prepare Coconut Filling and Crème Fraîche Frosting. To assemble, cut cake layers in half horizontally to make four layers. Place the first layer on a serving plate, cut side up. Spread one-third (about ¾ cup) of the Coconut Filling over the first cake layer. Repeat with two more layers and the remaining Coconut Filling. Top with the remaining cake layer. Frost top and sides of cake with Crème Fraîche Frosting. Top cake with coconut curls. Store cake, covered, in the refrigerator up to 24 hours. Makes 16 servings.

Coconut Filling In a medium saucepan combine 1¼ cups heavy cream, ¾ cup sugar, and ½ cup butter, cut up. Bring to boiling, stirring until sugar is dissolved. In a small bowl stir together 1 tablespoon cornstarch, 1 tablespoon water, and a dash salt. Stir into cream mixture; bring to boiling. Cook and stir 1 minute or until thickened. Remove from heat. Stir in 2 cups flaked or shredded coconut and ½ teaspoon vanilla. Transfer to a medium bowl. Cover surface with plastic wrap. Chill 2 hours.

COCONUT LAYER CAKE

GINGER-LIME ICEBOX CHEESECAKE

Crème Fraîche Frosting In a large bowl combine one 7-ounce container crème fraîche or one 8-ounce container sour cream, 1 cup heavy cream, ¾ cup powdered sugar, and ½ teaspoon vanilla. Beat with a mixer on medium until frosting is thick and soft peaks form (tips curl).

*Tip To toast coconut, preheat oven to 350°F. Spread coconut in a shallow baking pan. Bake 5 to 10 minutes or until just lightly browned around the edges, watching carefully to prevent burning.

PER SERVING *539 cal., 32 g fat (20 g sat. fat), 137 mg chol., 239 mg sodium, 61 g carb., 2 g fiber, 5 g pro.*

GINGER-LIME ICEBOX CHEESECAKE

PREP 20 minutes
CHILL 8 hours

6	limes
2	8-oz. pkg. cream cheese, softened
¾	cup powdered sugar
1	tsp. vanilla
2	cups heavy cream
1	16-oz. pkg. gingersnaps

1. Remove 2 tablespoons zest and squeeze ¾ cup juice from limes. In a large bowl combine 1 tablespoon of the zest, the juice, cream cheese, powdered sugar, and vanilla. Beat with a mixer on medium until smooth.

2. In another large bowl beat cream on medium until soft peaks form (tips curl). Fold whipped cream into cream cheese mixture.

3. Spread ½ cup of the cream mixture into a 9-inch springform pan and top with a single layer of cookies. Spread with 1½ cups cream mixture and top with another layer of cookies. Repeat layering twice. Spread with remaining cream mixture. Reserve any remaining cookies for garnish. Cover and chill 8 to 24 hours.

4. Remove sides of springform pan. Coarsely crush any remaining cookies and press onto sides of cheesecake. Top with remaining 1 tablespoon zest. Makes 12 servings.

PER SERVING *460 cal., 31 g fat (18 g sat. fat), 83 mg chol., 319 mg sodium, 41 g carb., 1 g fiber, 6 g pro.*

Ginger-Lemon Icebox Cheesecake For a lemon version, substitute lemon zest and juice for the lime zest and juice.

BREAD AND BUTTER PUDDING WITH SALTED CARAMEL WHISKEY BUTTER SAUCE

BREAD AND BUTTER PUDDING WITH SALTED CARAMEL WHISKEY BUTTER SAUCE

PREP 30 minutes
CHILL 30 minutes
BAKE 45 minutes at 375°F

⅔	cup raisins
½	cup Irish whiskey
5	eggs
2	cups heavy cream
1	cup sugar
½	tsp. ground cinnamon
¼	tsp. ground nutmeg
1	tsp. vanilla
8	1-inch slices country white bread (about 10 oz.) (crusts left on)
¾	cup unsalted butter, at room temperature
¼	cup unsalted butter, cubed
½	cup sugar
½	tsp. sea salt
1¼	cups heavy cream

1. For bread pudding, in a medium bowl combine the raisins and whiskey; let soak 1 hour. Butter a 2-quart rectangular baking dish; set aside.

2. For custard, in a large bowl whisk together the eggs, cream, sugar, cinnamon, nutmeg, and vanilla.

Generously spread one side of bread slices with the ¾ cup butter. Cut slices in half diagonally; arrange in the prepared baking dish, overlapping the slices. Drain raisins, reserving the whiskey. Sprinkle raisins on the bread, tucking some between slices. Pour custard over bread; cover with foil; refrigerate 30 minutes.

3. Preheat oven to 375°F. Place baking dish in a large roasting pan. Add hot water to halfway up the sides of dish. Bake 45 minutes or until pudding is set and top is golden (there will be a layer of melted butter over the pudding). Carefully remove baking dish; cool slightly on a wire rack (butter will soak into bread as it cools).

4. Meanwhile, for salted caramel whiskey butter sauce, melt the ¼ cup butter in a 2-quart saucepan over medium heat. Whisk in sugar, salt, cream, and 3 tablespoons of the reserved whiskey. Bring to boiling; reduce heat and simmer, uncovered, 10 to 15 minutes or until sauce thickens slightly, stirring frequently. Serve warm pudding with Salted Whiskey Sauce to spoon over. Makes 12 servings.

PER SERVING *585 cal., 42 g fat (25 g sat. fat), 207 mg chol., 242 mg sodium, 43 g carb., 1 g fiber, 6 g pro.*

BLACKBERRY AND POUND CAKE CRISP

PREP 25 minutes
BAKE 45 minutes at 350°F
STAND 15 minutes
COOL 15 minutes

1   10.75-oz. frozen pound cake, thawed
1   cup all-purpose flour
¾   cup packed brown sugar
½   tsp. ground cinnamon
¼   tsp. salt
⅓   cup butter, cut up
1   cup heavy cream
2   Tbsp. all-purpose flour
2   Tbsp. granulated sugar
4   cups fresh or frozen blackberries

1. Preheat broiler. Arrange an oven rack 4 inches from heat source. Cut pound cake into ½-inch slices. Place slices on baking sheet. Broil 1 minute per side or until lightly toasted. Cut toasted slices into fourths. Arrange pieces in a 2-quart rectangular baking dish. Preheat oven to 350°F.

2. For topping, in a medium bowl stir together the 1 cup flour, brown sugar, cinnamon, and salt. Using a pastry blender, cut in butter until mixture resembles coarse crumbs.

3. In a large bowl whisk cream, the 2 tablespoons flour, and granulated sugar until combined. Fold in blackberries. Spread blackberry mixture over pound cake layer. Sprinkle topping over blackberry mixture.

4. Bake 45 to 50 minutes or until topping is golden and filling is bubbly. Cool on a wire rack 15 minutes. Serve warm. Makes 6 servings.

PER SERVING *526 cal., 28 g fat (16 g sat. fat), 105 mg chol., 315 mg sodium, 66 g carb., 5 g fiber, 5 g pro.*

BLUEBERRY CRUMBLE SLAB PIE

PREP 30 minutes
BAKE 40 minutes at 375°F

2½   cups all-purpose flour
¾   tsp. salt
¾   cup butter-flavor shortening
8   to 10 Tbsp. ice water
1   cup sugar
¼   cup all-purpose flour
½   tsp. ground cinnamon
½   tsp. lemon zest
6   cups fresh or frozen blueberries*
1   recipe Crumb Topping

1. Preheat oven to 375°F. Line a 15×10-inch baking pan with foil, extending foil over edges of pan; set aside. For pastry, in a large bowl stir together 2½ cups flour and the salt. Using a pastry blender, cut in shortening until pieces are pea size. Sprinkle 1 tablespoon of the ice water over part of the flour mixture; toss gently with a fork. Push moistened pastry to side of bowl. Repeat moistening flour mixture, using 1 tablespoon ice water at a time, until all the pastry is moistened. Gather flour mixture into a ball, kneading gently until it holds together.

2. On a lightly floured surface, roll pastry into a 13×9-inch rectangle. Wrap pastry around the rolling pin; unroll into prepared baking pan. Ease pastry onto the bottom and up the sides without stretching. Trim pastry to ½ inch beyond edges of pan. Fold under extra pastry and crimp edges as desired.

3. In a large bowl stir together sugar, ¼ cup flour, the cinnamon, and lemon zest. Add blueberries; toss gently to coat. Spoon blueberry filling evenly into pastry-lined baking pan. Sprinkle with Crumb Topping.

4. Bake 40 to 45 minutes or until filling is bubbly and topping is golden. If necessary to prevent overbrowning cover top of pie loosely with foil the last 10 minutes of baking. Slightly cool pie in pan on a wire rack. Serve warm or cool completely. Use foil to lift uncut bars out of pan. Cut into bars. Makes 24 servings.

***Tip** If using frozen blueberries, toss with the sugar mixture as directed, then let stand at room temperature 30 minutes before adding to the pastry-lined pan. Berries will still be icy.

Crumb Topping In a large bowl stir together 1 cup rolled oats, 1 cup packed brown sugar, and ½ cup all-purpose flour. Using a pastry blender, cut in ½ cup butter until oat mixture resembles coarse crumbs. Stir in ½ cup chopped pecans.

PER SERVING *267 cal., 12 g fat (4 g sat. fat), 10 mg chol., 103 mg sodium, 38 g carb., 2 g fiber, 3 g pro.*

BLACKBERRY AND POUND CAKE CRISP

BLUEBERRY
CRUMBLE
SLAB PIE

CHOCOLATE-PEANUT
BUTTER CHEESECAKE

CHOCOLATE-PEANUT BUTTER CHEESECAKE

PREP 35 minutes
BAKE 53 minutes at 350°F
COOL 2 hours
CHILL 4 hours

3   8-oz. pkg. cream cheese
3   eggs
2   cups finely crushed peanut butter-filled peanut sandwich cookies
¼   cup butter, melted
12 oz. semisweet chocolate, chopped
1   cup heavy cream
½   cup creamy peanut butter
1¼ cups packed brown sugar
2   tsp. vanilla
15 miniature chocolate-covered peanut butter cups, halved or coarsely chopped

1. Allow cream cheese and eggs to stand at room temperature 30 minutes. Meanwhile, preheat oven to 350°F. For crust, in a medium bowl combine crushed cookies and melted butter. Press mixture onto the bottom and 1½ inches up the sides of a 9-inch springform pan. Bake 8 minutes. Cool on a wire rack.
2. For the chocolate layer, in a small saucepan combine chocolate and cream. Heat over low heat until chocolate is melted and mixture is smooth, stirring frequently. Pour 1½ cups of the chocolate mixture into crust-lined pan, spreading evenly. Chill in the freezer 10 minutes.
3. For the peanut butter layer, in a large bowl beat cream cheese and peanut butter with a mixer on medium to high until smooth. Beat in brown sugar until combined. Using a fork, lightly beat eggs. Add eggs to cream cheese mixture, beating just until combined. Stir in vanilla. Pour cream cheese mixture over chocolate layer in pan.
4. Bake 45 minutes or until a 2½-inch area around outside edge appears set when gently shaken. Cool in pan on a wire rack 15 minutes. Using a small sharp knife, loosen crust from sides of pan. Cool 30 minutes more. Remove sides of pan. Cool cheesecake completely on wire rack.
5. Spread the remaining chocolate mixture over top of cheesecake. Top with peanut butter cups. Cover and chill at least 4 hours or overnight before serving. Makes 12 servings.

CRANBERRY-WALNUT TART

PER SERVING *746 cal., 53 g fat (27 g sat. fat), 146 mg chol., 397 mg sodium, 64 g carb., 3 g fiber, 12 g pro.*

CRANBERRY-WALNUT TART

PREP 30 minutes
BAKE 28 minutes at 400°F
STAND 30 minutes

1¼ cups all-purpose flour
¾   cup plus 1 Tbsp. sugar
4   tsp. orange zest
⅓   cup butter, cut up
3   Tbsp. ice water
1¼ cups coarsely chopped walnuts
½   cup heavy cream
1   tsp. vanilla
2¼ cups fresh cranberries
2   oranges, peeled and sectioned

1. Preheat oven to 400°F. In a large bowl combine the flour, 1 tablespoon sugar, and 2 teaspoons orange zest. Cut in butter with a pastry blender until fine crumbs form. Stir in ice water. Use your hands to gather dough together.

2. Press dough into bottom and sides of a foil-lined 14×5-inch or 9-inch-round tart pan with removable bottom. Place pan on a foil-lined baking sheet. Bake 7 to 8 minutes or just until set. Transfer to wire rack. Spread walnuts evenly over crust.
3. Meanwhile, for filling, in a medium saucepan combine cream and ½ cup of the sugar. Bring to boiling, stirring to dissolve sugar. Cook and stir 1 minute. Remove from heat. Stir in vanilla. Pour over walnuts in crust. Bake 20 minutes or until top is browned. Remove and cool on a wire rack.
4. For topper, in a food processor add 2 cups of the cranberries, orange sections, remaining ¼ cup sugar, and 2 teaspoons zest. Pulse three to five times or until coarsely chopped. Stir in remaining ¼ cup whole cranberries. Let stand 30 minutes, stirring occasionally. Use foil to lift tart from pan to platter. Spoon cranberry topper over tart before serving. Makes 10 servings.
PER SERVING *282 cal., 14 g fat (4 g sat. fat), 15 mg chol., 8 mg sodium, 36 g carb., 3 g fiber, 4 g pro.*

CAPPUCCINO MERINGUE TART

PREP 1 hour
BAKE 7 minutes at 375°F
CHILL 3 hours
COOK 15 minutes

   Nonstick cooking spray
1   cup finely crushed amaretti cookies (about 4½ oz.)
½   cup ground almonds
2   Tbsp. sugar
⅓   cup butter, melted
⅓   cup sugar
1   Tbsp. plus 1 tsp. cornstarch
1   cup whole milk
½   cup heavy cream
¼   tsp. fine sea salt
3   large egg yolks, lightly beaten
1   Tbsp. hot water
¾   tsp. instant espresso powder*
1   tsp. vanilla
7   Tbsp. sugar
3   large egg whites
⅛   tsp. fine sea salt
½   tsp. vanilla

1. For the crust, preheat oven to 375°F. Lightly coat a 14×4½-inch rectangular (or 10-inch round) tart pan with removable bottom with cooking spray. Set aside.
2. In a medium bowl stir together crushed cookies, ground almonds, and 2 tablespoons sugar. Drizzle butter over mixture; toss until evenly coated. Spread in prepared pan; press evenly onto bottom and up sides. Bake 7 to 8 minutes or until edges are golden. Cool completely on a wire rack.
3. For cappuccino custard, in a medium-size heavy saucepan combine ⅓ cup sugar and cornstarch. Stir in milk, cream, and salt. Cook and stir over medium heat until thickened and bubbly. Cook and stir 2 minutes more. Remove from heat. Gradually stir 1 cup of the milk mixture into the three egg yolks.
4. Add egg mixture to remaining milk mixture in saucepan. Bring to a gentle boil; reduce heat. Cook and stir for 2 minutes. Remove from heat.
5. In a small cup stir together the hot water, instant espresso powder, and vanilla until espresso is dissolved. Whisk into custard.
6. Pour hot custard through a fine-mesh strainer into the tart shell; discard solids. Cover tart with plastic wrap, press wrap to surface of custard. Refrigerate until firm, at least 3 hours or up to 1 day.
7. For meringue topping, in the top of a 3-quart double boiler, combine 7 tablespoons sugar, egg whites, and salt. Beat with a mixer on low 30 seconds. Place pan over boiling water (top pan should not touch water). Cook, beating constantly on low, 3 to 5 minutes or until an instant-read thermometer registers 160°F. (Stop beaters and quickly scrape bottom and sides of pan occasionally to prevent sticking.) Remove pan from heat. Beat on high 5 minutes or until soft peaks form (tips curl). Add vanilla; beat until spreading consistency, about 2 minutes.
8. Using a piping bag fitted with a large round or star tip, pipe meringue in 1-inch kisses over the custard. Use a kitchen torch to toast meringue until deeply golden all over. (Alternatively, place tart pan on a baking sheet, then place under a broiler set to high 1 minute, watching closely to prevent burning.) Serve as soon as possible for best texture; store leftovers in the refrigerator. Makes 10 servings.
*Tip Instant espresso powder is a very dark and finely ground instant coffee. You can substitute regular instant coffee crystals.
PER SERVING *292 cal., 16 g fat (8 g sat. fat), 88 mg chol., 171 mg sodium, 32 g carb., 1 g fiber, 5 g pro.*

BITTERSWEET CHOCOLATE TART

PICTURED ON PAGE 77.

PREP 25 minutes
BAKE 14 minutes at 400°F
STAND 12 minutes
COOL 1 hour

½   cup butter, melted
¼   cup sugar
1   tsp. vanilla bean paste or vanilla extract
   Pinch salt
1   cup all-purpose flour
1   cup half-and-half
2   Tbsp. sugar
7   oz. 60% to 70% bittersweet chocolate, finely chopped
1   egg
   Sweetened whipped cream and fresh berries (optional)

1. Preheat oven to 400°F.
2. For pastry, in a medium bowl stir together melted butter, the ¼ cup sugar, vanilla paste, and salt. Stir in flour (dough will seem a little oily). Press pastry evenly into a 9-inch fluted tart pan with removable bottom. Place tart pan on a baking sheet. Bake 14 to 16 minutes or until golden; if needed to prevent over-browning cover edges with foil the last 5 minutes. Transfer tart on baking sheet to a wire rack.
3. Meanwhile, for filling, in a medium saucepan bring half-and-half and

CAPPUCCINO MERINGUE TART

2 tablespoons sugar to a simmer over medium-low heat, stirring occasionally. Simmer, stirring constantly, 3 minutes. Remove from heat. Add chopped chocolate, stirring constantly, until chocolate is melted and mixture is smooth. (It will look curdled at first but should become smooth and glossy as chocolate melts; if flecks remain after stirring, return pan to low heat for a moment to finish melting.)

4. In a medium bowl whisk egg until foamy. Whisk 2 tablespoons of the warm (not hot) chocolate mixture into the egg. Drizzling slowly, whisk in the remaining chocolate mixture.

5. Immediately pour filling into the warm crust. Return baking sheet with tart to oven; turn off oven. Let the tart stand in hot oven 12 to 13 minutes or until filling sets around edges and center 4 inches jiggle when gently shaken.

6. Transfer to a wire rack to cool completely before removing from pan (about 1 hour). If desired, serve with sweetened whipped cream or berries. Makes 8 servings.

PER SERVING *375 cal., 25 g fat (15 g sat. fat), 64 mg chol., 137 mg sodium, 36 g carb., 2 g fiber, 5 g pro.*

PEANUT BUTTER CHIFFON PIE

PREP 45 minutes
BAKE 8 minutes at 350°F
CHILL 3 hours

1½	cups finely crushed melba toasts
⅓	cup unsalted butter, melted
2	Tbsp. sugar
½	tsp. plus ⅛ tsp. fine sea salt
¼	cup cold water
2	tsp. unflavored gelatin
3	large egg yolks
1	cup sugar
⅔	cup whole milk
⅔	cup well-stirred, smooth, salted natural peanut butter
1	tsp. vanilla
1	cup plus ¾ cup heavy cream
¼	cup chopped roasted, salted peanuts

1. Preheat oven to 350°F. For crust, in a medium bowl combine crushed toasts, butter, 2 tablespoons sugar, and ¼ teaspoon of the salt. Stir to evenly coat. Press mixture onto bottom and sides of a 9-inch pie plate. Bake

PEANUT BUTTER CHIFFON PIE

8 minutes or until lightly golden. Cool completely on a wire rack.

2. For the peanut butter filling, in a small bowl whisk together the water and gelatin. Let stand 10 minutes.

3. Meanwhile, in a medium-size heavy-bottom saucepan, whisk together egg yolks, 1 cup sugar, milk, and ¼ teaspoon of the salt. Cook, stirring constantly, over medium heat until custard thickens and begins to bubble. Remove from heat; add gelatin mixture. Whisk until gelatin has dissolved and mixture is smooth. Whisk in peanut butter, vanilla, and remaining ⅛ teaspoon salt. Cool to room temperature.

4. In a large bowl beat 1 cup of the cream with a mixer on medium-high until stiff peaks form (tips stand straight). Fold about one-third of the whipped cream into the peanut butter filling. Gently fold in the remaining whipped cream until just a few streaks of white remain. Gently spoon filling into cooled pie crust. Chill at least 3 hours or up to overnight.

5. In a large bowl beat the remaining ¾ cup cream with a mixer on medium-high until soft peaks form. Spoon whipped cream over filling, then top with peanuts. Makes 10 servings.

PER SERVING *495 cal., 34 g fat (16 g sat. fat), 121 mg chol., 314 mg sodium, 39 g carb., 2 g fiber, 10 g pro.*

COCONUT CREAM
BANANA-TOPPED PIE

COCONUT CREAM BANANA-TOPPED PIE

PREP 50 minutes
BAKE 14 minutes at 450°F
CHILL 4 hours

1   recipe Pastry for Single-Crust Pie
¾   cup sugar
3   Tbsp. cornstarch
2   cups half-and-half or light cream
¾   cup plus 2 Tbsp. cream of coconut
4   egg yolks, lightly beaten
1   Tbsp. butter
1½ tsp. vanilla
1   cup unsweetened flaked coconut
½   cup heavy cream
4   oz. cream cheese, softened
3   medium bananas
     Raw chip coconut, toasted (tip, page 83)

1. Preheat oven to 450°F. Prepare Pastry for Single-Crust Pie. On a lightly floured surface, use your hands to slightly flatten pastry. Roll pastry from center to edges into a 12-inch diameter circle. Wrap pastry circle around rolling pin. Unroll into a 9-inch pie plate. Ease pastry into pie plate without stretching. Trim pastry to ½ inch beyond edge of pie plate. Fold under extra pastry even with plate edge. Crimp edge as desired. Generously prick bottom and sides of pastry with a fork. Line pastry with a double thickness of foil. Bake 8 minutes. Remove foil. Bake 6 minutes or until golden. Cool on a wire rack.
2. For filling, in a medium saucepan combine sugar and cornstarch. Gradually stir in half-and-half and ½ cup

of the cream of coconut. Cook and stir over medium-high heat until thickened and bubbly; reduce heat. Cook and stir 2 minutes more. Remove from heat. Gradually stir about 1 cup of the hot mixture into egg yolks. Return egg yolk mixture to saucepan. Bring to a gentle boil, stirring constantly; reduce heat. Cook and stir 2 minutes. Remove from heat. Stir in butter and 1 teaspoon of the vanilla until butter is melted. Stir in flaked coconut. Transfer filling to prepared pastry shell. Cover surface with plastic wrap and chill 4 to 6 hours or until filling is set and thoroughly chilled.
3. In a small bowl beat heavy cream with a mixer on medium to high until stiff peaks form (tips stand straight); set aside. In a medium bowl beat cream cheese on medium until smooth. Gradually beat in the 2 tablespoons cream of coconut. Fold in whipped cream. Spread cream cheese mixture over filling in pastry shell.
4. Just before serving, cut bananas into ¼- to ½-inch pieces; arrange on pie. For glaze, in a small bowl combine the remaining ¼ cup cream of coconut and ½ teaspoon vanilla. Spoon glaze over banana pieces. Sprinkle with toasted coconut. Serve immediately. Makes 8 servings.

Pastry for Single-Crust Pie In a medium bowl stir together 1½ cups all-purpose flour and ½ teaspoon salt. Using a pastry blender, cut in ¼ cup shortening and ¼ cup butter, cut up (or ½ cup shortening) until pieces are pea size. Sprinkle 1 tablespoon ice water over part of the flour mixture; toss gently with a fork. Push moistened pastry to side of bowl. Repeat moistening flour mixture, using 1 tablespoon ice water at a time, until all the flour mixture is moistened (¼ to ⅓ cup ice water total). Gather into a ball, kneading gently until it holds together.
PER SERVING 794 cal., 53 g fat (35 g sat. fat), 170 mg chol., 310 mg sodium, 76 g carb., 5 g fiber, 9 g pro.

BROWNIE WAFFLES À LA MODE

PREP 40 minutes
FREEZE 8 hours
COOK 1 minute per batch

1   qt. vanilla ice cream
½   cup crushed striped round peppermint candies*

2   oz. unsweetened chocolate, chopped
¼   cup butter
½   cup all-purpose flour
¼   cup unsweetened cocoa powder
¼   tsp. baking powder
¼   tsp. baking soda
¼   tsp. salt
2   eggs, lightly beaten
⅔   cup sugar
¼   cup half-and-half or light cream
1   tsp. vanilla
½   tsp. instant espresso coffee powder (optional)
     Nonstick cooking spray
     Chocolate fudge ice cream topping
     Crushed striped round peppermint candies (optional)

1. In a large chilled bowl combine ice cream and ½ cup crushed candies. Stir with a wooden spoon just until combined. Cover and freeze 8 hours or until firm.
2. In a small saucepan stir unsweetened chocolate and butter over low heat until melted; cool.
3. In a medium bowl stir together flour, cocoa powder, baking powder, baking soda, and salt. Make a well in the center of flour mixture; set aside. In a small bowl combine eggs, sugar, half-and-half, vanilla, espresso powder (if using), and cooled melted chocolate mixture. Add egg mixture all at once to flour mixture. Stir just until moistened (batter should be slightly lumpy).
4. Preheat a 7½-inch round waffle baker; lightly coat surface with cooking spray. Spoon a scant ½ cup batter onto grids of preheated waffle baker. Close lid quickly; do not open until done. Bake 1 minute or until waffle is cooked through. (Waffle will not be crisp; do not overcook). When done, use a fork to lift waffle off grid. Cool on a wire rack. Repeat with remaining batter.
5. Separate waffles into quarters; serve with ice cream in dessert bowls. Drizzle with fudge topping and, if desired, sprinkle with additional crushed candies. Makes 10 servings.
*Tip If you like, omit the peppermint candies and use coffee, butter pecan, or strawberry ice cream.
PER SERVING 396 cal., 21 g fat (12 g sat. fat), 113 mg chol., 313 mg sodium, 49 g carb., 1 g fiber, 6 g pro.

BROWNIE WAFFLES
À LA MODE

TOASTED COCONUT
ICEBOX CAKE WITH
CARAMEL AND
FUDGE

BOOZY ORANGE CRÈME BRÛLÉE

PREP 25 minutes
COOK 35 minutes
BAKE 1 hour at 350°F
COOL 2 hours 30 minutes
CHILL 2 hours

1½	cups sugar
1	cup cold water
2	mandarin oranges or oranges
4	to 5 kumquats
1¼	cups heavy cream
1½	cups milk
2	Tbsp. whiskey
6	eggs
1	Tbsp. vanilla
2	to 3 Tbsp. sugar

1. Adjust oven rack to center position; preheat oven to 350°F. Place a 9-inch deep-dish pie plate (use ceramic if you will broil topping in Step 7) in a large roasting pan; set aside.
2. For caramel, in a small saucepan combine ¾ cup sugar and the cold water over medium-low heat. Heat 5 minutes or until sugar is dissolved, stirring constantly. Increase heat; bring to boiling. Cook without stirring 25 to 30 minutes or until golden. Remove from heat; cool 2 minutes. Pour into pie plate.
3. Meanwhile, zest one mandarin; set zest aside. (Reserve mandarin for another use.) Slice remaining mandarin and all kumquats ⅛ inch thick; set aside.
4. In a medium saucepan combine cream, milk, whiskey, and zest over medium heat. Heat 8 to 10 minutes or until bubbles form at sides of saucepan, stirring occasionally; remove from heat.
5. In a medium bowl whisk eggs and remaining ¾ cup sugar until pale and creamy, about 30 seconds. Whisk half the cream mixture into egg mixture. Slowly pour egg mixture into remaining cream mixture, whisking constantly. Whisk in vanilla. Slowly pour into pie plate.
6. Pour boiling water into roasting pan around pie plate to a depth of 1 inch. Bake 1 hour or until set, topping with reserved citrus slices the last 20 minutes of baking. Cool on a wire rack 30 minutes. Cover; chill at least 2 hours or overnight.

TOASTED COCONUT ICEBOX CAKE WITH CARAMEL AND FUDGE

PREP 30 minutes
CHILL 8 hours
BAKE 5 minutes at 350°F

1	cup shredded coconut
2	14-oz. cans unsweetened coconut milk,* unshaken and chilled overnight
1	cup heavy cream
½	cup powdered sugar
1	tsp. vanilla
1	6.75- to 7.5-oz. pkg. crisp caramel or square shortbread cookies (24 to 28)
1	Tbsp. hot fudge-flavor ice cream topping, warmed
1	Tbsp. caramel-flavor ice cream topping
	Shaved or shredded coconut, toasted (tip, page 83)

1. Preheat oven to 350°F. Spread 1 cup coconut in a 15×10-inch baking pan. Bake 5 minutes or until toasted, shaking pan once or twice; cool.
2. Scrape hardened coconut cream from top of coconut milk into a large bowl (reserve coconut liquid for smoothies). Beat coconut cream with a mixer until smooth. Add cream, powdered sugar, and vanilla. Beat on medium-high until stiff peaks form (tips stand straight).
3. To assemble, line an 8×4-inch loaf pan with plastic wrap, extending wrap over edges. Spread ¼ cup of the whipped cream into prepared loaf pan. Top with a single layer of cookies, ¾ cup whipped cream, and ¼ cup coconut. Repeat layering cookies, whipped cream, and coconut three more times. Cover with plastic wrap and chill 8 to 24 hours. Cover and chill remaining whipped cream.
4. To serve, unmold cake onto a platter. Generously frost top with remaining whipped cream. Drizzle servings with fudge and caramel toppings and sprinkle with shaved coconut. Makes 8 servings.
*Tip Use a brand of coconut milk, such as Thai Kitchen or Geisha, that contains guar gum so the coconut cream will beat to a smooth and creamy consistency.

7. For brûlée, after chilling, sprinkle top of custard with 2 to 3 tablespoons granulated sugar. Use a culinary torch to melt and caramelize the sugar. Or, preheat broiler. Adjust an oven rack to 5 inches from heat source. Sprinkle top of custard with 2 to 3 tablespoons sugar. Broil 4 minutes, rotating pan, or until sugar is evenly caramelized. Makes 8 servings.

PER SERVING *378 cal., 18 g fat (11 g sat. fat), 185 mg chol., 88 mg sodium, 45 g carb., 1 g fiber, 8 g pro.*

MEYER LEMON POTS DE CREME

PREP 30 minutes
BAKE 35 minutes at 325°F
COOL 30 minutes
CHILL 4 hours

⅔   cup sugar
1½   tsp. Meyer lemon zest
¼   cup Meyer lemon juice
     Dash salt
¾   cup heavy cream
3   egg yolks, lightly beaten
2   Tbsp. honey
3   kumquats, thinly sliced

1. Preheat oven to 325°F. Place four 4-ounce pots de crème pots, ramekins, or 6-ounce custard cups in a 2-quart square baking pan; set aside.
2. In a small saucepan combine sugar, lemon zest, lemon juice, and salt. Slowly stir in cream. Cook and stir over medium heat just until simmering.
3. In a medium bowl lightly whisk egg yolks. Slowly whisk hot cream mixture into egg yolks. Divide mixture among pots.
4. With baking pan on oven rack, carefully pour enough hot water into baking pan to halfway up sides of pots. Bake 35 minutes or until edges of custards are set and centers jiggle slightly when shaken. Transfer to wire racks; cool 30 minutes. Cover and chill 4 hours or up to 2 days before serving.
5. In a small skillet combine honey and thinly sliced kumquat. Cook and stir over low heat 3 minutes or until honey is melted and kumquats soften slightly and glaze. Cool slightly. Spoon over pots de creme. Makes 4 servings.

PER SERVING *372 cal., 20 g fat (12 g sat. fat), 200 mg chol., 62 mg sodium, 47 g carb., 1 g fiber, 3 g pro.*

BOOZY ORANGE
CRÈME BRÛLÉE

MEYER LEMON
POTS DE CREME

Christmas Cookies and Bars

Ready, set, bake! It's the season for homemade cookies, bars, and treats of all kinds. Here's where you find inspiration.

MEXICAN CHOCOLATE-
DULCE DE LECHE
SANDWICH COOKIES,
PAGE 106

95

BLUEBERRY-SAGE
THUMBPRINTS

SALTED CARAMEL
THUMBPRINTS

BLUEBERRY-SAGE THUMBPRINTS

PREP 25 minutes
BAKE 10 minutes per batch at 350°F
COOL 1 minute

2 cups all-purpose flour
⅔ cup finely ground yellow cornmeal
1½ tsp. dried sage, crushed
¼ tsp. baking powder
¼ tsp. salt
1 cup butter, softened
1 cup packed brown sugar
2 egg yolks
2 tsp. lemon zest
1½ tsp. vanilla
¼ to ⅓ cup blueberry or blackberry preserves
  Fresh blueberries

1. Preheat oven to 350°F. In a medium bowl combine flour, cornmeal, sage, baking powder, and salt. Set aside.
2. In a large bowl beat butter with a mixer on medium 30 seconds. Add brown sugar and beat until combined, scraping sides of bowl occasionally. Beat in egg yolks, lemon zest, and vanilla until combined. Beat in as much of the flour mixture as you can with the mixer. Stir in remaining flour mixture.

3. Shape dough into ¾-inch balls. Place 1 inch apart on a cookie sheet. Lightly press the tip of your thumb into the center of each ball. Fill centers with ¼ teaspoon blueberry preserves. Bake 10 minutes or until edges are set and bottoms are lightly browned. Cool on cookie sheet 1 minute; transfer to a wire rack; cool completely. Top cookies with fresh blueberries. Makes 50 servings.
PER SERVING *81 cal., 4 g fat (2 g sat. fat), 17 mg chol., 49 mg sodium, 11 g carb., 0 g fiber, 1 g pro.*

SALTED CARAMEL THUMBPRINTS

PREP 40 minutes
BAKE 12 minutes per batch at 350°F
COOL 5 minutes

2 cups all-purpose flour
⅔ cup sugar
1 cup butter
½ tsp. vanilla
16 vanilla caramels, unwrapped
⅓ cup heavy cream
3 oz. bittersweet chocolate, coarsely chopped
½ tsp. shortening
  Fleur de sel or other coarse salt

1. Preheat oven to 350°F. Line cookie sheets with parchment paper; set aside. In a large bowl combine flour and sugar. Using a pastry blender, cut in butter and vanilla until mixture resembles fine crumbs and starts to cling. Form into a ball, kneading until smooth.
2. Shape dough into 1-inch balls. Place balls 2 inches apart on prepared cookie sheets. Lightly press the tip of your thumb in the center of each ball. Bake 12 to 14 minutes or until edges are lightly browned. If cookie centers puff during baking, re-press centers with rounded side of measuring teaspoon. Cool on cookie sheets 5 minutes. Remove; cool on wire racks.
3. In a small heavy saucepan combine caramels and heavy cream. Heat over low heat until caramels melt, stirring constantly. Spoon a scant teaspoon into each indentation.
4. In a small saucepan heat and stir chocolate and shortening until melted and smooth. Drizzle over cooled cookies and sprinkle with salt. Makes 32 servings.
PER SERVING *124 cal., 7 g fat (5 g sat. fat), 19 mg chol., 89 mg sodium, 14 g carb., 0 g fiber, 1 g pro.*

LEMON-GINGER SNOWBALLS

FROZEN COCONUT-COFFEE BITES

LEMON-GINGER SNOWBALLS

PREP 30 minutes
CHILL 1 hour
BAKE 10 minutes at 350°F
COOL 2 minutes

½   cup shortening
1   Tbsp. grated fresh ginger or finely chopped crystallized ginger
1   Tbsp. vanilla
2   tsp. honey-lemon-ginseng flavor green tea (loose tea from 1 bag)
1   tsp. lemon zest
1   cup packed brown sugar
2   tsp. ground ginger
1   tsp. baking powder
½   tsp. baking soda
¼   tsp. salt
2   large eggs
2½ cups all-purpose flour
    Granulated sugar
1   recipe Powdered Sugar Glaze
    White nonpareils and lemon zest

1. In large bowl beat shortening, ginger, vanilla, tea, and lemon zest on medium until fluffy. Add brown sugar; beat until well-combined. Beat in ground ginger, baking powder, baking soda, and salt. Beat in eggs. Beat in as much flour

as you can; stir in remaining by hand. Refrigerate dough 1 hour or until easy to handle.
2. Preheat oven to 350°F. Shape dough in 1-inch balls. Roll in granulated sugar and place on two ungreased baking sheets.
3. Bake 10 minutes or until lightly browned around edges. Cool 2 minutes on baking sheets. Transfer to wire racks to cool completely. Dip in powdered sugar glaze; sprinkle with nonpariels and lemon zest. Let stand on waxed paper to dry. Makes 48 servings.
Powdered Sugar Glaze In a small bowl stir together 1 cup powdered sugar and 4 teaspoons water until thick drizzling consistency.
PER SERVING *75 cal., 2 g fat (1 g sat. fat), 9 mg chol., 35 mg sodium, 13 g carb., 0 g fiber, 1 g pro.*

FROZEN COCONUT-COFFEE BITES

PREP 30 minutes
FREEZE 4 hours 10 minutes

¼   cup unsalted butter
1   cup sweetened shredded coconut
2   Tbsp. finely crushed graham crackers
1½   tsp. instant espresso coffee powder or 2 tsp. instant coffee crystals

2½   Tbsp. boiling water
5   oz. cream cheese, softened
5   Tbsp. sugar
½   tsp. ground cinnamon
     Dash salt
½   tsp. vanilla
     Chocolate-covered coffee beans (optional)

1. Line an 8-inch square baking pan with nonstick foil, extending foil over the edges.
2. For crust, in a medium nonstick skillet melt butter over medium-low heat. Add coconut; cook and stir until golden. Stir in crushed graham crackers. Remove from heat; cool slightly. Press into the prepared pan. Freeze 10 minutes.
3. Dissolve espresso powder in boiling water. In a bowl beat cream cheese with a mixer on medium until smooth and creamy. Beat in sugar, cinnamon, and salt. Beat in vanilla and espresso.
4. Spread cream cheese mixture over crust. Freeze at least 4 hours before serving. Sprinkle with chocolate-covered coffee beans if desired. Makes 20 servings.
PER SERVING *62 cal., 5 g fat (3 g sat. fat), 12 mg chol., 30 mg sodium, 4 g carb., 0 g fiber, 1 g pro.*

LADY BALTIMORE TASSIES

PREP 30 minutes
STAND 10 minutes
BAKE 25 minutes at 325°F
COOL 5 minutes

½ cup butter, softened
1 3-oz. pkg. cream cheese, softened
¾ cup all-purpose flour
¼ cup ground pecans or walnuts
¼ cup orange juice
2 Tbsp. orange liqueur (such as Grand Marnier) or orange juice
3 Tbsp. finely chopped dried Calimyrna (light) figs
2 Tbsp. golden raisins, finely chopped
1 egg, lightly beaten
¾ cup packed brown sugar
Dash salt
⅓ cup chopped pecans or walnuts
1 recipe Meringue Frosting
Finely chopped pecans or walnuts

1. Preheat oven to 325°F. For pastry, in a small bowl beat butter and cream cheese with a mixer on medium until combined. Stir in flour and ¼ cup ground nuts. If necessary, cover and chill dough 30 minutes or until easy to handle. Shape dough into 24 balls. Press each ball into the bottom and up the sides of 24 ungreased 1¾-inch muffin cups.

2. For filling, in a small saucepan combine orange juice, orange liqueur, figs, and raisins. Bring just to boiling; remove from heat. Let stand 10 minutes to soften figs and raisins. Drain off and discard any liquid. In a small bowl stir together the egg, brown sugar, and salt. Stir in ⅓ cup chopped nuts, drained figs, and raisins. Spoon a heaping teaspoon of filling into each pastry-lined cup.

3. Bake 25 to 30 minutes or until pastry is golden. Cool in pan on a wire rack 5 minutes. Run a knife around muffin cups to loosen tassies. Carefully transfer to a wire rack; cool completely.

4. Just before serving, prepare Meringue Frosting. Spoon frosting into a pastry bag fitted with a ½-inch round tip. Pipe frosting onto tassies. Sprinkle with finely chopped nuts. Makes 24 servings.

Meringue Frosting In a small mixing bowl beat ¼ cup sugar, 2 tablespoons water, 1 tablespoon pasteurized liquid egg whites (or 1 teaspoon meringue powder), ½ teaspoon vanilla, and ⅛ teaspoon cream of tartar with a mixer on high 3 to 5 minutes until stiff peaks form (tips stand straight).

PER SERVING 136 cal., 8 g fat (3 g sat. fat), 22 mg chol., 58 mg sodium, 15 g carb., 1 g fiber, 1 g pro.

LADY BALTIMORE TASSIES

SUGAR COOKIES

PREP 40 minutes
CHILL 30 minutes
BAKE 7 minutes per batch at 375°F

1 cup butter, softened
1¼ cups sugar
1½ tsp. baking powder
½ tsp. salt
2 eggs
2 tsp. vanilla
3 cups all-purpose flour
1 recipe Royal Icing (optional)

1. In a large bowl beat butter with a mixer on medium 30 seconds. Add sugar, baking powder, and salt. Beat until combined, scraping bowl as needed. Beat in eggs and vanilla. Beat in flour. Divide dough in half. Cover and

SUGAR COOKIES

chill 30 minutes or until dough is easy to handle.

2. Preheat oven to 375°F. On a lightly floured surface, roll one portion of dough at a time to ⅛- to ¼-inch thickness. Using 2½-inch cookie cutters, cut dough shapes. Place 1 inch apart on an ungreased cookie sheet.

3. Bake 7 minutes or until edges are firm and bottoms are very light brown. Remove; cool on a wire rack. If desired,

decorate with Royal Icing. Makes 52 servings.

PER SERVING *80 cal., 4 g fat (2 g sat. fat), 17 mg chol., 63 mg sodium, 10 g carb., 0 g fiber, 1 g pro.*

Royal Icing In a large bowl stir together one 16-ounce package (about 4 cups) powdered sugar, 3 tablespoons meringue powder,* and ½ teaspoon cream of tartar. Add ½ cup warm water and 1 teaspoon vanilla. Beat with a

mixer on low until combined. Beat on high 7 to 10 minutes or until stiff piping consistency. Use icing immediately or cover bowl with a damp paper towel; cover tightly with plastic wrap. Chill up to 48 hours. Makes about 5 cups.

*Tip Look for meringue powder in the baking aisle of large supermarkets or in the cake decorating department of hobby and crafts stores.

SPIKED TRUFFLES

SPIKED TRUFFLES

PREP 30 minutes
CHILL 1 hour 30 minutes
STAND 30 minutes

1   12-oz. pkg. semisweet chocolate
    chips or one 11.5-oz. pkg. milk
    chocolate chips
⅓   cup heavy cream
4   tsp. salted caramel Irish cream
    liqueur, such as Baileys; hazelnut
    liqueur; or milk
    Coatings, such as unsweetened
    dark and/or regular cocoa
    powder, luster dust, and/or gold
    glitter crystals

1. In a medium-size heavy saucepan
combine chocolate chips and cream.
Stir constantly over low heat until melted.
Cool slightly. Stir in liqueur. Beat chocolate
mixture with a mixer on low until smooth.
Chill 1½ to 2 hours or until firm.
2. Line a tray or baking sheet with
waxed paper. Shape chocolate mixture
into ¾- to 1-inch balls. Roll balls in
coatings; place on prepared tray. Let
stand 30 minutes before serving. Makes
25 servings.
PER SERVING *90 cal., 6 g fat (3 g sat.
fat), 4 mg chol., 2 mg sodium, 10 g carb.,
1 g fiber, 1 g pro.*

CHOCOLATE-PISTACHIO TREES

PREP 45 minutes
CHILL 30 minutes
COOL 15 minutes
BAKE 9 minutes per batch at 350°F

1   cup butter
⅔   cup packed brown sugar
1   tsp. vanilla
1   egg, beaten
2¼ cups all-purpose flour
¼   cup unsweetened cocoa powder
¾   cup finely chopped pistachio nuts
¾   cup semisweet chocolate pieces
1   Tbsp. shortening
½   cup ground pistachio nuts

1. In a medium saucepan heat and stir butter and brown sugar over low heat until butter is melted. Remove saucepan from heat; stir in vanilla. Cool 15 minutes. Stir in egg, flour, and cocoa powder until mixture is combined. Stir in the ¾ cup pistachio nuts. Divide dough in half. Cover and chill 30 minutes or until dough is easy to handle.

2. Preheat oven to 350°F. On a lightly floured surface, roll dough, half at a time, to ¼-inch thickness. Use a tree-shape cookie cutter to cut out cookies. Place cookies 1 inch apart on an ungreased cookie sheet.

3. Bake 9 minutes or until edges are firm. Transfer to a wire rack; cool.

4. In a heavy saucepan heat and stir chocolate pieces and shortening over low heat until chocolate is melted. Remove from heat. Dip one-third of each cookie into chocolate mixture; roll edge in ground nuts. Makes 48 servings.

PER SERVING *105 cal., 7 g fat (3 g sat. fat), 15 mg chol., 44 mg sodium, 9 g carb., 1 g fiber, 2 g pro.*

GINGERSNAP SHORTBREAD

PREP 30 minutes
BAKE 18 minutes at 325°F

2   cups all-purpose flour
½   cup powdered sugar
½   tsp. ground ginger
¼   tsp. ground cinnamon
⅛   tsp. ground cloves
1   cup butter
2   Tbsp. molasses
     Granulated sugar
     Red hot hearts (optional)

1. Preheat oven to 325°F. In a large bowl stir together flour, powdered sugar, ginger, cinnamon, and cloves. Using a pastry blender, cut in butter until mixture resembles fine crumbs. Drizzle with molasses; toss gently. Form dough into a ball and knead until smooth. Divide dough in half.

2. On an extra-large ungreased cookie sheet (or two small cookie sheets) pat or roll each portion of dough into an 8-inch circle. Make scalloped edges then sprinkle with granulated sugar. Cut each circle into eight wedges (do not separate wedges). Prick with a fork. If desired, use a small heart-shape cookie cutter to make impressions on wedges.

3. Bake 18 to 20 minutes just until bottoms start to brown and centers are set. Cut circles into wedges again while warm. Cool on wire racks. If desired, pipe a dot of frosting in the center of each shortbread; lightly press a heart on the frosting. Makes 16 servings.

PER SERVING *183 cal., 12 g fat (7 g sat. fat), 31 mg chol., 93 mg sodium, 18 g carb., 0 g fiber, 2 g pro.*

CHOCOLATE-PISTACHIO TREES

GINGERSNAP SHORTBREAD

CINNAMON CRUNCH
SNICKERDOODLES

CINNAMON CRUNCH SNICKERDOODLES

PREP 30 minutes
CHILL 30 minutes
BAKE 10 minutes per batch at 375°F
COOL 2 minutes

1   cup butter, softened
1½   cups sugar
1   tsp. baking soda
1   tsp. cream of tartar
¼   tsp. salt
2   eggs
1   tsp. vanilla
3   cups all-purpose flour
4½   cups sweetened cinnamon
     toast-flavor wheat and rice
     cereal, such as Cinnamon Toast
     Crunch

1. In a large bowl beat butter with
a mixer on medium 30 seconds.
Add sugar, baking soda, cream of
tartar, and salt. Beat until combined,
scraping bowl as needed. Beat in
eggs and vanilla. Beat in flour. Stir in
1 cup of the cereal. Cover; chill 30 to
60 minutes or until dough is easy
to handle.
2. Preheat oven to 375°F. Place
remaining 3½ cups cereal in a
resealable plastic bag; crush with a
rolling pin. Shape dough into 1¼-inch
balls. Roll balls in crushed cereal;
place 2 inches apart on an ungreased
cookie sheet.
3. Bake 10 to 12 minutes or until
bottoms are lightly browned. Cool on
cookie sheet 2 minutes. Remove; cool
on a wire rack. Makes 48 servings.
PER SERVING *106 cal., 4 g fat (3 g
sat. fat), 18 mg chol., 99 mg sodium,
15 g carb., 0 g fiber, 1 g pro.*

SPRITZ CHRISTMAS COOKIE WREATH

PREP 30 minutes
BAKE 7 minutes per batch at 375°F

1½   cups butter
1   cup sugar
1   tsp. baking powder
1   egg
2   tsp. vanilla
1   tsp. almond extract
3½   cups all-purpose flour
3   Tbsp. rainbow nonpareils
     Green food color
     Peppermint candies

SPRITZ CHRISTMAS COOKIE WREATH

1. Preheat oven to 375°F. In a large bowl beat butter with a mixer on medium to high 30 seconds. Add sugar and baking powder. Beat until combined, scraping bowl as needed. Beat in egg, vanilla, and almond extract until combined. Beat in flour. Knead in sprinkles and food coloring to desired color.

2. Place dough, in batches, into cookie press fitted with star plate. Force dough through cookie press onto an ungreased cookie sheet. Bake 7 to 9 minutes or until edges are firm and just starting to brown. Remove; cool completely on wire racks.

3. In a 12×2-inch round dish stack cookies in a wreath shape; fill center with candies. Makes 84 servings.
PER SERVING *59 cal., 3 g fat (2 g sat. fat), 11 mg chol., 33 mg sodium, 7 g carb., 0 g fiber, 1 g pro.*

CHOCOLATE-COCONUT MACAROONS

PREP 30 minutes
BAKE 15 minutes at 325°F
STAND 25 minutes

- 2 egg whites
- ½ tsp. vanilla
- ⅛ tsp. cream of tartar
  Dash salt
- ⅔ cup sugar
- ¾ cup shredded coconut
- 2 oz. dark chocolate or semisweet chocolate, coarsely grated

1. Preheat oven to 325°F. Line two cookie sheets with parchment paper; set aside. In a large bowl beat egg whites, vanilla, cream of tartar, and salt with a mixer on high until soft peaks form (tips curl). Gradually add sugar, about 1 tablespoon at a time, beating until stiff peaks form (tips stand straight). Gently fold in ½ cup of the coconut and the chocolate.
2. Drop 2 tablespoons batter each into 18 mounds on the prepared cookie sheets, about 1 inch apart. Sprinkle tops with remaining ¼ cup coconut. Place cookie sheets on separate oven racks.

CHOCOLATE-COCONUT MACAROONS

3. Bake 15 minutes. Rotate cookie sheets top to bottom and forward to back. Turn off oven; let macaroons dry in oven 25 minutes. Transfer to a wire rack to cool. Makes 18 servings.
PER SERVING *72 cal., 3 g fat (2 g sat. fat), 0 mg chol., 28 mg sodium, 11 g carb., 1 g fiber, 1 g pro.*

POPPY SEED CROISSANT COOKIES

PREP 40 minutes
CHILL 1 hour 45 minutes
BAKE 15 minutes per batch at 350°F

- 1 8-oz. pkg. cream cheese, softened
- 1 cup butter, softened
- ¼ cup granulated sugar
- 2 tsp. lemon zest
- 1 tsp. vanilla
- ¼ tsp. salt
- 2 cups all-purpose flour
- 1 12.5-oz. can poppy seed pastry and dessert filling
- 2 Tbsp. granulated sugar
- 1 egg
- 1 Tbsp. milk
- 1 to 2 Tbsp. powdered sugar (optional)

1. In a large bowl beat cream cheese, butter, and the ¼ cup granulated sugar with a mixer on medium to high until light and fluffy. Beat in 1 teaspoon of the lemon zest, the vanilla, and salt. Add flour; beat on low just until combined.
2. Turn dough out onto a lightly floured surface; divide into four equal portions. Shape each portion into a ball. Cover and chill dough 1 hour or until easy to handle. Meanwhile, in a medium bowl stir together poppy seed filling, the 2 tablespoons sugar, and remaining 1 teaspoon lemon zest.
3. Line cookie sheets with parchment paper; set aside. On a lightly floured surface, roll one portion of dough at a time into a 9-inch circle. Spoon about ¼ cup of the poppy seed filling onto the circle; spread to ½ inch from edges. Using a sharp knife, cut circle into 12 wedges. Starting at a wide edge, roll up each wedge. Place 2 inches apart on prepared cookie sheets, point sides down. Repeat with remaining dough and filling. Cover and chill 45 minutes.
4. Preheat oven to 350°F. In a small bowl whisk together egg and milk until frothy. Lightly brush on cookies. Bake 15 to 18 minutes or until tops are light golden

POPPY SEED CROISSANT COOKIES

brown. Transfer to a wire rack to cool completely. Use a fine-mesh strainer to lightly sift powdered sugar over cookies. Makes 48 servings.

PER SERVING *102 cal., 6 g fat (3 g sat. fat), 19 mg chol., 68 mg sodium, 10 g carb., 0 g fiber, 1 g pro.*

CHERRY-ALMOND HALF MOONS

PREP 45 minutes
CHILL 1 hour 30 minutes
BAKE 12 minutes per batch at 375°F

1   cup butter, softened
1   8-oz. pkg. cream cheese, softened
1   tsp. almond extract
2   cups all-purpose flour
½   cup cherry preserves
2   egg whites
1   recipe Almond Icing
     Toasted, sliced almonds

1. In a large bowl beat butter and cream cheese with a mixer on medium to high 30 seconds. Beat in almond extract until combined. Beat in flour until dough comes together. Divide dough in half. Cover; chill dough 1½ hours or until easy to handle.

2. Preheat oven to 375°F. Line cookie sheets with parchment paper. On a lightly floured surface, roll half the dough at a time to ⅛-inch thickness. Using a 3-inch round scalloped-edge cookie cutter, cut out dough. Place rounds 1 inch apart on prepared cookie sheets.

3. Spoon ½ teaspoon cherry preserves onto one side of each round; spread to ¼ inch from edge. Fold dough rounds in half, enclosing preserves; press edges with tines of a fork to seal. Whisk egg whites until frothy; lightly brush cookies with egg whites.

4. Bake 12 to 15 minutes or until cookies are lightly browned. Transfer cookies to a wire rack to cool completely. Drizzle cookies with Almond Icing. Sprinkle with almonds. Let stand until icing is set. Makes 32 servings.

Almond Icing In a small bowl stir together ¾ cup powdered sugar, ¼ teaspoon almond extract, and enough water (1 to 2 tablespoons) to make drizzling consistency icing.

PER SERVING *134 cal., 9 g fat (5 g sat. fat), 23 mg chol., 79 mg sodium, 13 g carb., 0 g fiber, 2 g pro.*

CHERRY-ALMOND HALF MOONS

MOCK TOFFEE

PREP 15 minutes
CHILL 1 hour

10 graham cracker squares
⅓ cup chopped almonds
½ cup packed brown sugar
½ cup butter
⅓ cup miniature semisweet chocolate pieces

1. Line a microwave-safe 2-quart rectangular baking dish with parchment paper, extending paper over edges of dish. Place graham crackers in a single layer in the dish, breaking crackers as necessary to fit. Sprinkle crackers with almonds.
2. Combine brown sugar and butter in a 4-cup microwave-safe glass measure or medium bowl. Microwave, uncovered, on high 3 minutes or just until melted, stirring every 30 seconds. Quickly pour over crackers and nuts in dish.
3. Microwave, uncovered, 1½ minutes. Sprinkle with chocolate pieces. Chill 1 to 2 hours or until chocolate is set. Use parchment paper to lift toffee from dish. Cut into squares. Makes 12 servings.
PER SERVING *177 cal., 11 g fat (6 g sat. fat), 20 mg chol., 92 mg sodium, 18 g carb., 0 g fiber, 1 g pro.*

MEXICAN CHOCOLATE-DULCE DE LECHE SANDWICH COOKIES

PREP 30 minutes
CHILL 2 hours
BAKE 8 minutes per batch at 325°F
COOL 2 minutes

3 cups all-purpose flour
½ cup unsweetened dark cocoa powder
1 tsp. ground cinnamon
1 tsp. baking powder
1 tsp. baking soda
½ tsp. salt
1 cup butter, softened
1 cup granulated sugar
½ cup packed brown sugar
2 eggs
1 Tbsp. vanilla
1 13.4-oz. can dulce de leche

1. In a medium bowl stir together flour, cocoa powder, cinnamon, baking powder, baking soda, and salt; set aside. In a large bowl combine butter, granulated sugar, and brown sugar. Beat with a mixer on medium until light and fluffy. Add eggs and vanilla; beat until combined, scraping sides of bowl occasionally. Beat in as much of the flour mixture as you can with the mixer. Using a wooden spoon, stir in any remaining flour mixture. Divide dough in half. Cover and chill 2 hours or until dough is easy to handle.
2. Preheat oven to 325°F. Line cookie sheets with parchment paper; set aside. On a lightly floured surface, roll half the dough at a time to ¼-inch thickness. Using a 3-inch round scalloped-edge cookie cutter, cut out dough. Place cutouts 1 inch apart on prepared cookie sheets. Using a 1-inch round scalloped-edge cookie cutter, cut centers of half the cutouts.
3. Bake 8 to 10 minutes or until firm when lightly pressed with a finger. Cool on cookie sheets 2 minutes. Transfer to a wire rack; cool completely.
4. For each sandwich cookie, spread about 2 teaspoons dulce de leche on the flat side of a cookie without center cutout. Top with a cookie with cutout center, bottom side down. Makes 26 servings.
PER SERVING *219 cal., 9 g fat (5 g sat. fat), 37 mg chol., 200 mg sodium, 32 g carb., 1 g fiber, 3 g pro.*

MOCK TOFFEE

MEXICAN CHOCOLATE-
DULCE DE LECHE
SANDWICH COOKIES

HAZELNUT
SHORTBREAD
SANDWICH COOKIES

PREP 30 minutes
FREEZE 30 minutes
BAKE 12 minutes per batch at 350°F

2   cups all-purpose flour
1   cup hazelnuts, coarsely chopped
½   tsp. salt
1   cup unsalted butter, softened

¾   cup powdered sugar
½   cup chocolate-hazelnut spread
2   to 4 Tbsp. heavy cream

1. In a food processor combine flour, ½ cup of the chopped hazelnuts, and the salt. Cover and process about 1 minute or until nuts are finely ground. Transfer flour mixture to a medium bowl. In the processor combine butter and powdered sugar. Cover and process until smooth. Add flour mixture.

Cover and pulse just until a dough forms, scraping down sides of bowl as necessary. Add remaining ½ cup chopped hazelnuts. Cover and pulse until combined. Divide dough in half. Shape each half into an 8-inch log. Wrap each log in plastic wrap or waxed paper. Freeze 30 minutes or until firm.
2. Preheat oven to 350°F. Line a large cookie sheet with parchment paper. Cut logs into ¼-inch slices. Place slices 1 inch apart on prepared cookie sheet.

Bake 12 to 15 minutes or just until edges are golden. Cool on cookie sheet on wire rack.

3. For ganache, in a small bowl microwave the chocolate-hazelnut spread about 1 minute or until warm, stirring once. Stir in 2 tablespoons cream. If necessary, stir in additional cream, 1 teaspoon at a time, to reach spreading consistency.

4. Spread 1 teaspoon ganache on half the cookie bottoms. Top with remaining cookies, bottom sides down. Drizzle sandwich cookies with the remaining ganache (thin with additional cream if necessary). Makes 25 servings.

PER SERVING *188 cal., 13 g fat (6 g sat. fat), 21 mg chol., 51 mg sodium, 16 g carb., 1 g fiber, 2 g pro.*

CHIPOTLE-CHOCOLATE SANDWICH BITES

PREP 30 minutes
CHILL 1 hour
BAKE 6 minutes per batch at 350°F
COOL 2 minutes

- 9 oz. Mexican-style sweet chocolate or semisweet chocolate, chopped
- 2 Tbsp. heavy cream
- 1 Tbsp. butter
- ¼ cup butter, softened
- ¼ cup shortening
- 2 oz. cream cheese, softened
- 1 cup packed brown sugar
- ½ to 1 tsp. ground chipotle chile pepper
- ½ tsp. baking powder
- ½ tsp. salt
- ½ tsp. ground cinnamon
- ¼ tsp. ground nutmeg
- 1 egg
- 2 tsp. vanilla
- 2½ cups all-purpose flour
  Ground chipotle chile pepper (optional)

1. For filling, in a small heavy saucepan stir 6 ounces of the chocolate, the cream, and 1 tablespoon butter over low heat until chocolate is melted. Transfer to a medium bowl. Cover; chill 1 hour or until nearly firm. Beat with a mixer on medium to high until light and fluffy.

2. Preheat oven to 350°F. Line a cookie sheet with parchment paper; set aside. In a large bowl beat the ¼ cup softened butter, the shortening, and cream cheese on medium to high 30 seconds.

CHIPOTLE-CHOCOLATE SANDWICH BITES

Add brown sugar, ½ teaspoon ground chipotle pepper, baking powder, salt, cinnamon, and nutmeg. Beat until combined, scraping sides of bowl occasionally. Beat in egg and vanilla until combined. Beat in as much of the flour as you can with the mixer. Use a spoon to stir in any remaining flour and remaining 3 ounces chocolate.

3. Shape dough into 1-inch balls. Place balls 1 inch apart on prepared cookie sheet. Using the bottom of a glass, flatten balls to ¼-inch thickness. If desired, sprinkle with additional ground chipotle pepper.

4. Bake 6 to 8 minutes or until edges are set. Cool on cookie sheet 2 minutes.

Transfer cookies to a wire rack; cool completely.

5. Spread filling onto bottoms of half the cookies. Top with remaining cookies, bottom sides down. Makes 25 servings.

To Store Layer sandwich cookies between sheets of waxed paper in an airtight container; cover. Store at room temperature up to 3 days or freeze up to 3 months.

PER SERVING *177 cal., 7 g fat (4 g sat. fat), 18 mg chol., 90 mg sodium, 26 g carb., 1 g fiber, 2 g pro.*

CHOCOLATE-COFFEE WHOOPIE PIES WITH COFFEE CREAM

PREP 40 minutes
BAKE 10 minutes per batch at 350°F
COOL 2 minutes

½   cup shortening
1   cup granulated sugar
1   tsp. baking soda
¼   tsp. salt
1   egg
3   Tbsp. instant espresso coffee powder or instant coffee crystals
2   tsp. vanilla
2½ cups all-purpose flour
⅔   cup unsweetened cocoa powder
1¼ cups buttermilk
¾   cup butter, softened
2   cups powdered sugar
¼   cup unsweetened cocoa powder
1   to 2 Tbsp. plus 1 tsp. milk

1. Preheat oven to 350°F. In a large bowl beat shortening with a mixer on medium 30 seconds. Add granulated sugar, baking soda, and salt. Beat until combined. Add egg, 2 tablespoons espresso powder, and 1 teaspoon vanilla. Beat until combined. In a medium bowl stir together the flour and ⅔ cup cocoa powder. Alternately add flour mixture and buttermilk to butter mixture, beating on low after each addition just until combined.
2. Drop dough from a rounded measuring tablespoon 2½ inches apart onto parchment lined cookie sheets. Bake 10 minutes or until edges are firm. Cool on cookie sheets 2 minutes. Transfer cookies to wire racks. Cool completely.
3. For the coffee cream, in a large bowl beat the butter with a mixer on medium-high 30 seconds. Beat in powdered sugar and ¼ cup cocoa powder. Set aside. In a small bowl combine remaining 1 tablespoon espresso powder, 1 teaspoon milk, and remaining 1 teaspoon vanilla. Stir until espresso is dissolved. Beat espresso mixture into butter mixture. Add 1 to 2 tablespoons milk, if necessary, to reach spreading consistency.
4. To assemble, spread half the cookie bottoms with about 1½ tablespoons coffee cream; top with remaining cookies. Makes 20 servings.
PER SERVING *272 cal., 13 g fat (6 g sat. fat), 29 mg chol., 174 mg sodium, 38 g carb., 2 g fiber, 3 g pro.*

CHOCOLATE-COFFEE WHOOPIE PIES WITH COFFEE CREAM

SALTED CARAMEL BROWNIES WITH PRETZEL CRUST

PREP 25 minutes
BAKE 40 minutes at 350°F

½   cup all-purpose flour
1   cup crushed pretzels
½   cup packed brown sugar
¼   tsp. baking soda
½   cup butter, melted
7   oz. unsweetened chocolate, coarsely chopped
¾   cup butter
¼   cup water
1   cup granulated sugar
¾   cup packed brown sugar
2   eggs
1   tsp. vanilla

1⅓ cups all-purpose flour
⅛ tsp. salt
⅛ tsp. ground cinnamon
2 to 3 oz. chocolate, melted
10 to 13 caramel candies, melted
    Fleur de sel

1. Preheat oven to 350°F. For crust, stir together the first four ingredients (through baking soda). Stir in ½ cup melted butter. Pat crust into ungreased 8-inch square baking pan. Bake 10 minutes.
2. In a medium saucepan combine chocolate, butter, and water. Stir constantly over low heat until chocolate is melted. Transfer to a large bowl.
3. Add granulated sugar and brown sugar to chocolate mixture; beat with mixer on low to medium until combined. Add eggs and vanilla; beat on medium 2 minutes. Add flour, salt, and cinnamon. Beat on low until combined. Spread batter on crust in pan.
4. Bake 30 to 35 minutes or until a toothpick inserted near center comes out clean. Cool in pan on a wire rack.
5. For drizzle, place melted chocolate and melted caramel in separate resealable plastic bags. Snip off a corner of each bag. Drizzle caramel then chocolate over brownies. Sprinkle with fleur de sel. Makes 20 servings.
Make Ahead Prepare brownies as directed; do not cut into bars. Cover pan. Store at room temperature up to 3 days. For longer storage, cut brownies into bars and layer between waxed paper in an airtight container; cover. Freeze up to 3 months. Thaw brownies; add drizzle.
PER SERVING *353 cal., 19 g fat (11 g sat. fat), 50 mg chol., 219 mg sodium, 43 g carb., 2 g fiber, 4 g pro.*

**SALTED CARAMEL BROWNIES
WITH PRETZEL CRUST**

BUTTERY MACADAMIA-CRUSTED COCONUT-PINEAPPLE BARS

PREP 30 minutes
BAKE 40 minutes at 350°F

2   cups all-purpose flour
¾   cup macadamia nuts, finely chopped
½   cup packed brown sugar
6   Tbsp. butter
1   20-oz. can crushed pineapple (juice pack), undrained
4   eggs
2   cups granulated sugar
1   cup flaked coconut
½   cup all-purpose flour
1   tsp. baking powder
1   tsp. rum extract or brandy extract
½   tsp. salt
1   cup powdered sugar

1. Preheat oven to 350°F. Grease a 13×9-inch baking pan; set aside. For crust, in a food processor combine 2 cups flour, macadamia nuts, and brown sugar. Cover and pulse until well mixed. Add butter. Cover and pulse until mixture starts to cling. Evenly press mixture onto bottom of prepared baking pan. Bake 10 minutes. Remove from oven.
2. Meanwhile, drain pineapple, reserving juice for glaze. In a medium bowl beat eggs with a fork until frothy. Stir in pineapple, granulated sugar, coconut, ½ cup flour, baking powder, rum extract, and salt until combined.
3. Evenly pour pineapple filling over hot crust. Bake 30 to 35 minutes or until bubbly and golden. Cool in pan on wire rack.
4. For glaze, in a small bowl stir together powdered sugar and 1 to 2 tablespoons reserved pineapple juice to reach drizzling consistency. Drizzle glaze over uncut bars. Let stand until glaze is set. Cut into bars. Makes 36 servings.
PER SERVING *164 cal., 5 g fat (2 g sat. fat), 26 mg chol., 78 mg sodium, 28 g carb., 1 g fiber, 2 g pro.*

BUTTERY MACADAMIA-CRUSTED COCONUT-PINEAPPLE BARS

PEANUT BUTTER BROWNIES

PREP 30 minutes
BAKE 30 minutes at 350°F

4   oz. bittersweet chocolate, coarsely chopped
¼   cup butter
¼   cup peanut butter
1   cup packed brown sugar
2   eggs
1   tsp. vanilla
⅔   cup all-purpose flour
¼   tsp. baking soda
⅛   tsp. salt
1   cup chopped chocolate-covered peanut butter cups
1   recipe Nutty Frosting Chocolate-covered peanut butter cups, halved or quartered (optional)

1. In a medium saucepan combine bittersweet chocolate, butter, and peanut butter. Stir over low heat until melted; cool slightly. Preheat oven to 350°F. Line an 8×8-inch baking pan with foil, extending foil over edges of pan. Grease foil; set pan aside.
2. Stir brown sugar into chocolate mixture. Add eggs, one at a time, beating with a wooden spoon after each addition just until combined. Stir in vanilla. In a small bowl stir together flour, baking soda, and salt. Add flour mixture to chocolate mixture; stir just until combined. Stir in the 1 cup chopped peanut butter cups. Pour batter into the prepared baking pan, spreading evenly.
3. Bake 30 minutes or until set. Cool in pan on wire rack. Cut into bars. Pipe or spoon Nutty Frosting in the center of each bar. If desired, top with halved mini peanut butter cups. Makes 24 servings.
Nutty Frosting In a medium bowl combine ½ cup peanut butter; ½ cup butter, softened; 1 tablespoon milk; and 1 teaspoon vanilla. Beat with a mixer on medium until combined. Gradually beat in 2 cups powdered sugar.
PER SERVING *252 cal., 14 g fat (6 g sat. fat), 33 mg chol., 134 mg sodium, 30 g carb., 1 g fiber, 4 g pro.*

PEANUT BUTTER
BROWNIES

**CRANBERRY-
CANDIED GINGER
BLONDIES WITH
TOASTED
MACADAMIAS**

CRANBERRY-CANDIED GINGER BLONDIES WITH TOASTED MACADAMIAS

PREP 30 minutes
COOL 15 minutes
BAKE 28 minutes at 350°F

16	oz. white baking chocolate with cocoa butter, chopped
½	cup butter, cut up
3	eggs, lightly beaten
½	cup sugar
1¾	cups all-purpose flour
1	tsp. vanilla
1	cup macadamia nuts, coarsely chopped
½	cup dried cranberries, snipped
¼	cup finely chopped crystallized ginger
1	Tbsp. shortening
	Snipped dried cranberries (optional)

1. Preheat oven to 350°F. Line a 13×9-inch baking pan with foil, extending foil over edges of pan. Lightly grease foil; set pan aside.
2. In a medium saucepan stir 12 ounces of the white chocolate over low heat until melted. Remove from heat. Stir in butter until melted. Cool 15 minutes.
3. Whisk eggs and sugar into white chocolate mixture until smooth. Stir in flour and vanilla just until combined. Fold in nuts, ½ cup dried cranberries, and 2 tablespoons of the ginger. Spread batter evenly in prepared baking pan.
4. Bake 28 to 30 minutes or until top is lightly browned and edges start to pull away from sides of pan. Cool in pan on wire rack.
5. In a small saucepan heat remaining 4 ounces white chocolate and shortening over low heat until melted, stirring constantly. Drizzle over uncut bars. Sprinkle with remaining 2 tablespoons ginger and, if using, additional dried cranberries. Use edges of foil to lift uncut bars out of pan. Cut into bars. Makes 32 servings.
PER SERVING *191 cal., 11 g fat (6 g sat. fat), 30 mg chol., 48 mg sodium, 19 g carb., 1 g fiber, 3 g pro.*

TOFFEE-PUMPKIN PIE BARS

MAPLE-NUT PIE BARS

TOFFEE-PUMPKIN PIE BARS

PREP 30 minutes
BAKE 40 minutes at 375°F

2   cups crushed gingersnaps
¼   cup granulated sugar
¼   cup all-purpose flour
½   cup butter, melted
1   15-oz. can pumpkin
¾   cup packed brown sugar
1   tsp. ground cinnamon
¾   tsp. ground ginger
½   tsp. salt
¼   tsp. ground cloves
1½   cups half-and-half
4   eggs, lightly beaten
½   cup almond toffee bits
½   cup chopped pecans, toasted (tip, page 34)
     Caramel-flavor ice cream topping (optional)

1. Preheat oven to 375°F. Grease a 13×9-inch baking pan. For crust, in a medium bowl combine gingersnaps, sugar, and flour. Stir in melted butter. Press mixture onto bottom of prepared pan.

2. In a large bowl combine next six ingredients (through cloves). Stir in half-and-half and eggs just until combined. Spread batter in crust-lined pan.
3. Bake 40 to 45 minutes or until a knife inserted near center comes out clean. Sprinkle with toffee bits and pecans. Cool in pan on wire rack. Cut into bars. Cover and chill within 2 hours. If desired, drizzle with caramel topping before serving. Makes 32 servings.
PER SERVING *145 cal., 8 g fat (4 g sat. fat), 41 mg chol., 139 mg sodium, 17 g carb., 1 g fiber, 2 g pro.*

MAPLE-NUT PIE BARS

PREP 25 minutes
BAKE 40 minutes at 350°F

     Nonstick cooking spray
1½   cups all-purpose flour
⅔   cup powdered sugar
¼   tsp. salt
⅔   cup butter
3   eggs, lightly beaten
1¼   cups chopped mixed nuts or pecans
¾   cup packed brown sugar
¾   cup pure maple syrup
3   Tbsp. butter, melted
½   tsp. maple flavoring or 1 tsp. vanilla

1. Preheat oven to 350°F. Line a 13×9-inch baking pan with foil, extending foil over edges. Lightly coat foil with cooking spray.
2. For crust, in a medium bowl stir together flour, powdered sugar, and salt. Using a pastry blender, cut in ⅔ cup butter until mixture resembles coarse crumbs. Press mixture onto bottom of prepared pan. Bake 20 minutes or until lightly browned.
3. Meanwhile, for filling, in another medium bowl combine remaining ingredients. Spread filling over hot crust.
4. Bake 20 minutes or until filling is set. Cool in pan on wire rack. Using foil, lift out uncut bars. Cut into bars. If desired, drizzle with additional maple syrup before serving. Makes 24 servings.
PER SERVING *203 cal., 11 g fat (5 g sat. fat), 41 mg chol., 113 mg sodium, 25 g carb., 1 g fiber, 3 g pro.*

Gifts from the Kitchen

Package yummy homemade treats to deliver throughout the season. Your thoughtfulness and the treats will be warmly greeted.

CHIPPERS in a jar

TOFFEE-PECAN CHIPPERS IN A JAR, PAGE 119

CARAMEL APPLE BREAD
PUDDING, PAGE 127

ACCORDION
CHEESE BREAD

ACCORDION CHEESE BREAD

PREP 45 minutes
RISE 1 hour 30 minutes
BAKE 40 minutes at 350°F

1¼ cups milk
⅓ cup butter
⅓ cup sugar
1 tsp. salt
1 pkg. active dry yeast
1 egg
4 to 4¼ cups all-purpose flour
¼ cup butter, melted
1 Tbsp. Dijon mustard
¼ tsp. bottled hot pepper sauce
1 cup finely shredded sharp
   cheddar cheese (4 oz.)
½ cup finely chopped green onions (4)

1. In a medium saucepan combine the milk, butter, sugar, and salt. Heat over low heat until warm (105°F to 115°F). Remove from heat. Stir in yeast until dissolved. In a large bowl lightly beat the egg with a fork. Add the milk mixture and 1½ cups of the flour. Beat with a mixer on low 1 minute, scraping sides of bowl constantly.

2. Using a wooden spoon, stir in enough of the remaining flour to make a soft dough that just starts to pull away from the sides of the bowl (dough will be slightly sticky). Transfer dough to a large lightly greased bowl. Cover; let rise in a warm place until nearly double in size (1 to 1½ hours).

3. Punch dough down. Turn dough out onto a lightly floured surface. Divide dough in half. Cover; let rest 10 minutes. Meanwhile, lightly grease two 8×4-inch foil loaf pans. In a small bowl stir together the melted butter, mustard, and hot pepper sauce.

4. For each loaf, on a lightly floured surface, roll one dough half into a 20×12-inch rectangle. Brush with half the butter mixture. Sprinkle with half the cheese and onions. Cut the dough crosswise into six equal strips. Stack the strips. Cut the stacked strips crosswise into six equal pieces. Arrange stacked pieces next to each other, cut sides up, in a loaf pan.* Sprinkle any spilled cheese and onions on top and drizzle with remaining butter mixture. Cover; let rise in a warm place 30 minutes.

5. Preheat oven to 350°F. Bake 40 minutes, covering loaves with foil the last 15 minutes of baking to prevent overbrowning. Cool in pans on a wire rack. Wrap loaves in pans. Attach directions for reheating loaves. Makes 12 servings.

***Tip** To easily transfer stacked dough into the pan, tip the pan on a short side and use a spatula to transfer dough squares.

To Reheat Cover loaf with foil. Warm in a 350°F oven 30 minutes or until heated through. Remove from pan and pull bread apart to serve.

PER SERVING *236 cal., 10 g fat (6 g sat. fat), 38 mg chol., 288 mg sodium, 30 g carb., 1 g fiber, 6 g pro.*

TOFFEE-PECAN CHIPPERS IN A JAR

(PICTURED ON PAGE 116)

PREP 20 minutes
BAKE 8 minutes per batch at 350°F

1⅓ cups all-purpose flour
⅓ cup packed brown sugar
⅓ cup granulated sugar
½ tsp. baking soda
½ tsp. cream of tartar
¼ tsp. salt
⅔ cup bittersweet or semisweet
   chocolate pieces
½ cup toffee pieces
½ cup coconut
⅓ cup chopped pecans, toasted (tip,
   page 34)

1. In a 1-quart jar layer all ingredients in order listed. Fasten lid. Attach directions to make cookies. Store filled jar in a cool, dry place up to 1 month.

To Make Cookies Preheat oven to 350°F. Empty contents of jar into a large bowl. In another bowl whisk together 1 egg, ¼ cup softened butter, and ¼ cup vegetable oil. Add to flour mixture; stir until combined. Drop dough by rounded teaspoons 2 inches apart onto ungreased cookie sheets. Bake 8 to 10 minutes or until edges are lightly browned. Cool on cookie sheets 1 minute. Transfer cookies to wire racks to cool. Makes 30 servings.

PER SERVING *123 cal., 7 g fat (3 g sat. fat), 12 mg chol., 74 mg sodium, 14 g carb., 1 g fiber, 1 g pro.*

As a gift Place scrapbooking letter stickers (a) on a disposable foil pan lid (b) to spell "Enjoy." For the "o," use a round scrapbooking embellishment (c). Make a gift tag from a paper snowflake cutout (d) and ribbon (e).

As a gift Space and affix four photo corners (a) to a 1-quart jar (b) to hold a playing card (c). Squeeze glue onto the face side of playing card and slide it into photo corners; press to adhere. Center and glue a label (d) onto card. Tie a ribbon (d) around the lid.

CHEESY TOMATO
PARTY SNACK MIX

CHEESY TOMATO PARTY SNACK MIX

PREP 15 minutes
BAKE 30 minutes at 300°F
COOL 30 minutes

3   cups bite-size square corn cereal, puffed corn cereal, or oyster crackers
3   cups bite-size square rice cereal or 3 plain rice cakes, broken into bite-size pieces
3   cups bite-size square wheat cereal or round toasted oat cereal
1   cup salted roasted soy nuts or corn nuts
1   cup small pretzel knots, circles, or bite-size pretzel snaps
1   cup fish-shape cheddar cheese crackers
¼   cup olive oil or canola oil
2   Tbsp. dried Italian seasoning, crushed
2   Tbsp. grated Parmesan cheese
2   Tbsp. finely snipped dried tomato (not oil-packed)
1   Tbsp. reduced-sodium Worcestershire sauce
¼   tsp. freshly ground black pepper

1. Preheat oven to 300°F. In a large roasting pan combine the cereals, soy nuts, pretzels, and crackers; set aside.
2. In a small bowl stir together the oil, Italian seasoning, Parmesan cheese, tomato, Worcestershire sauce, and pepper. Pour oil mixture over cereal mixture in pan; toss until well coated.
3. Bake 30 minutes, stirring twice. Spread snack mix on a large sheet of foil to cool. Makes 24 servings.
PER SERVING *102 cal., 4 g fat (1 g sat. fat), 1 mg chol., 205 mg sodium, 15 g carb., 2 g fiber, 3 g pro.*

CINNAMON AND FRUIT COOKIES

PREP 30 minutes
BAKE 15 minutes per batch at 350°F
COOL 3 minutes

½   cup butter, softened
½   cup shortening
1½ cups packed brown sugar
2   tsp. ground cinnamon
¾   tsp. baking powder
½   tsp. salt
¼   tsp. baking soda
2   eggs
1   Tbsp. vanilla
1¾ cups all-purpose flour
3   cups regular rolled oats
1   cup dried cranberries
½   cup chopped pitted dates

1. Preheat oven to 350°F. Line cookie sheets with parchment paper; set aside. In an extra-large bowl beat butter and shortening with a mixer on medium to high 30 seconds. Add brown sugar, cinnamon, baking powder, salt, and baking soda. Beat until combined, scraping sides of bowl occasionally. Beat in eggs and vanilla until combined. Beat in the flour. Stir in the oats, raisins, and dates.
2. Use a scant ¼-cup measure to drop mounds of dough about 3 inches apart onto prepared cookie sheets. Bake 15 to 17 minutes or until lightly browned and centers appear set. Cool on cookie sheets 3 minutes. Transfer to a wire rack to cool. Place cookies in gift bags. Makes 25 servings.
PER SERVING *258 cal., 9 g fat (4 g sat. fat), 27 mg chol., 107 mg sodium, 40 g carb., 3 g fiber, 5 g pro.*

As a gift Reuse a glass wide-mouth bottle with lid (a). Fill the bottle with snack mix or crackers; cover. Tie on a ribbon (b) and attach jingle bells (c).

As a gift Line a small burlap gift bag (a) with brown parchment paper (b). Add cookies or snack mix to the parchment liner. Tie the bag closed with a ribbon (c) and attach a tag (d).

CINNAMON
AND FRUIT
COOKIES

mmm...
cookies

MINI ITALIAN QUICHES

PREP 40 minutes
BAKE 20 minutes at 375°F
COOL 5 minutes

1   recipe Pastry Dough
½   cup shredded Italian-style cheese blend
¼   cup finely chopped marinated artichoke hearts, well drained
¼   cup finely chopped pepperoni
1   Tbsp. snipped fresh parsley
1   tsp. all-purpose flour
¼   tsp. dried Italian seasoning, crushed
⅛   tsp. crushed red pepper
2   eggs
¾   cup half-and-half, light cream, or whole milk
    Snipped fresh parsley (optional)

1. Preheat oven to 375°F. Shape chilled Pastry Dough into twelve 1½-inch balls. Press each ball into the bottoms and up the sides of twelve 2½-inch muffin cups; set aside.

2. For filling, in a medium bowl stir together cheese, artichoke hearts, pepperoni, the 1 tablespoon parsley, the flour, Italian seasoning, and crushed red pepper. Spoon into pastry-lined cups. In the same bowl whisk together eggs and half-and-half. Spoon over filling.

3. Bake 20 to 25 minutes or until filling is set and edges of pastry are golden. Cool in pan on a wire rack 5 minutes. Run the tip of a thin knife around edges of each quiche; carefully remove from muffin cups. Cool completely on a wire rack. If desired, top with additional parsley. Wrap and include directions for reheating. Makes 12 servings.

To Reheat Preheat oven to 350°F. Place quiche cups in a shallow baking pan. Bake 15 to 18 minutes or until heated through.

Pastry Dough In a medium bowl stir together 1½ cups all-purpose flour and ¼ teaspoon salt. Using a pastry blender, cut in ½ cup cold butter, cut up, until pieces are pea size. Sprinkle 1 tablespoon ice water over part the flour mixture; toss gently with a fork. Push moistened pastry to one side of bowl. Repeat moistening flour mixture, using 1 tablespoon ice water at a time, until all of the flour mixture is moistened (3 to 4 tablespoons total). Gather flour mixture into a ball, kneading gently until it holds together. Cover and chill at least 1 hour.

PER SERVING *186 cal., 13 g fat (7 g sat. fat), 67 mg chol., 204 mg sodium, 13 g carb., 0 g fiber, 5 g pro.*

MINI ITALIAN QUICHES

GIANT CAPPUCCINO CRINKLES

PREP 30 minutes
CHILL 1 hour
BAKE 13 minutes per batch at 350°F
COOL 1 minute

- ⅔ cup butter, softened
- 2 cups packed brown sugar
- 1⅓ cups unsweetened cocoa powder
- 2 Tbsp. instant coffee granules
- 2 tsp. baking soda
- 2 tsp. ground cinnamon
- ¼ tsp. salt
- 4 egg whites
- 1 6-oz. carton vanilla low-fat yogurt
- 3 cups all-purpose flour
- ½ cup granulated sugar

1. In a large bowl beat butter with a mixer on medium-high 30 seconds. Add the next six ingredients (through salt). Beat until combined. Beat in the egg whites and yogurt. Beat in as much of the flour as you can with the mixer. Stir in any remaining flour. Cover; chill dough 1 hour or until easy to handle.

2. Preheat oven to 350°F. Place the granulated sugar in a small bowl. Shape dough into 2-inch balls; roll balls in sugar. Place balls 3 inches apart on an ungreased cookie sheet. Flatten slightly with the bottom of a glass.

3. Bake 13 to 15 minutes or until edges are firm. Cool cookie sheet 1 minute. Transfer to a wire rack to cool completely. Makes 24 servings.

PER SERVING *219 cal., 6 g fat (3 g sat. fat), 14 mg chol., 185 mg sodium, 38 g carb., 1 g fiber, 4 g pro.*

GIANT CAPPUCCINO CRINKLES

As a gift Wrap plastic forks (a) in holiday paper napkins (b) and tie together with twine (c). Place treats in a 9×9×2-inch white box lid (d). Place fork and napkin bundles with treats in lid. Tie a sheer ribbon (e) around the lid.

As a gift Cut a strip of scrapbooking paper (a) and adhere it around the tin (b) using crafts glue. Attach lettered game pieces (c) to the side of the tin. Using crafts glue, attach a ribbon (d) around the edge of the lid and a scalloped gift tag (e) to the top of the lid.

HAZELNUT ROCKY
ROAD BROWNIE MIX

HAZELNUT ROCKY ROAD BROWNIE MIX

PREP 15 minutes
BAKE 35 minutes at 325°F

1¼ cups sugar
⅔ cup unsweetened cocoa powder
2 oz. milk or dark chocolate, chopped (optional)
1 cup all-purpose flour
¼ tsp. baking soda
⅛ tsp. salt
¼ cup chopped, toasted* hazelnuts
⅓ cup tiny marshmallows
½ cup chocolate-hazelnut spread

1. In a 1-quart jar layer sugar, cocoa powder, and chopped chocolate (if using). In a small bowl stir together flour, baking soda, and salt. Spoon over chocolate in jar. Top with hazelnuts and marshmallows; attach lid. Attach directions to make brownies. Spoon chocolate-hazelnut spread into a 4-ounce jar or small resealable container to accompany brownie mix.

To Make Brownies Preheat oven to 325°F. Line a 9×9-inch baking pan with foil, extending foil over edges of pan. Grease the foil; set pan aside. Set aside chocolate-hazelnut spread. In a large bowl whisk together ⅔ cup melted butter and 3 eggs until well combined. Add jar contents to butter mixture; stir until well combined. Spread batter evenly in prepared pan. Bake 35 minutes or until a wooden toothpick inserted near center comes out with just a few crumbs. Cool brownies in pan on a wire rack. For frosting, in a medium bowl beat ¼ cup softened butter on low 30 seconds. Add ½ cup powdered sugar and beat until smooth. Beat in chocolate-hazelnut spread until smooth. If necessary, beat in 1 to 2 teaspoons milk for spreading consistency. Spread frosting on cooled brownies. Use foil to lift uncut brownies out of pan. Place on cutting board. Cut into bars. Makes 16 servings.

*Tip To toast hazelnuts, preheat oven to 350°F. Spread nuts in a shallow baking pan. Bake 8 to 10 minutes or until nuts are lightly toasted. Cool nuts slightly; place on a clean kitchen towel. Rub nuts with towel to remove loose skins.

PER SERVING *302 cal., 17 g fat (9 g sat. fat), 63 mg chol., 152 mg sodium, 36 g carb., 2 g fiber, 4 g pro.*

As a gift Apply velvet poinsettia stickers (a) to a quart jar (b). Glue a vintage foil flower (c) to a paper tag (d). Affix a large button (e) to center of flower with glue. Glue tag to lid.

APPLE-BERRY PIE IN A JAR

PREP 50 minutes
BAKE 40 minutes at 375°F

1 recipe Pastry
2 Tbsp. butter
1½ lb. apples and/or pears, peeled, cored, and chopped into ½-inch pieces
½ cup sugar
2 Tbsp. all-purpose flour
 Dash salt
1 cup raspberries and/or blueberries
 Milk
 Coarse or granulated sugar

1. Preheat oven to 375°F. Prepare Pastry. Divide the two-thirds portion into six equal portions. Place a portion into each of six 1-cup wide-mouth canning jars. Press the dough evenly onto the bottom and up the sides of each jar. Set jars aside.
2. In a large skillet melt butter over medium heat. Add apples; cook 5 to 8 minutes or until tender, stirring occasionally. Stir in the ½ cup sugar, the flour, and salt. Cook until slightly thickened. Remove from heat. Fold in raspberries. Spoon ½ cup fruit mixture into each pastry-lined jar.
3. On a lightly floured surface, roll the remaining one-third portion of pastry into a 13-inch circle. Using a 4-inch round cutter, cut out six pastry circles. Using a small cutter, cut shape in the center of each circle.
4. Place a pastry circle on fruit filling in each jar. Press pastry around inside of jar rim. Sprinkle pastry with coarse sugar. (Alternately, cut shapes from large pastry circle and arrange shapes on filling. Brush shapes with milk and sprinkle with sugar.)
5. Place jars in a 15×10×1-inch baking pan. Bake 40 to 45 minutes or until pastry is golden. Cool completely on wire rack. Makes 6 servings.
Pastry In a large bowl stir together 2½ cups all-purpose flour and 1 teaspoon salt. Using a pastry blender cut in ½ cup shortening and ¼ cup butter, cut up, until pieces are pea size. Sprinkle 1 tablespoon ice water over part of the flour mixture; toss with a fork. Push moistened pastry to side of bowl. Repeat moistening flour mixture, using 1 tablespoon ice water

at a time (½ to ⅔ cup total), until flour is moistened. Gather pastry into a ball, kneading gently until it holds together. Divide pastry into one-third and two-thirds portions.
Lattice Top Prepare as directed except cut the one-third portion of dough into ⅜-inch-wide strips instead of circles. Cut strips into 4-inch lengths. Place three strips across filling in each jar. Arrange three more strips perpendicular to first strips. Trim strips even with jar. Press strips into the pastry inside jar. Brush with milk and sprinkle with coarse sugar. Bake as directed.
PER SERVING *586 cal., 28 g fat (11 g sat. fat), 31 mg chol., 498 mg sodium, 77 g carb., 6 g fiber, 6 g pro.*

As a gift Bake pies in 1-cup wide-mouth canning jars (a). Place a cooled pie in a pint-size wooden berry basket (b). Wrap red yarn or twine (c) around the box several times on one side, then wrap yarn perpendicular along adjacent edge to prevent jar from slipping. Knot and clip yarn ends. Cut a small wedge from scrapbooking paper (d), label with recipe name, and tuck into yarn.

APPLE-BERRY PIE
IN A JAR

OATMEAL
JAM BARS

As a gift Line the bottom of a large rectangular gift box (a) with waxed paper. Place bars in the box. Affix ribbons (b) to the top of the box with glue. Write the name of the recipe with chalk on chalkboard cardstock (c) and attach to the box with glue.

OATMEAL JAM BARS

PREP 15 minutes
BAKE 35 minutes at 350°F

1⅓	cups all-purpose flour
¼	tsp. baking soda
¼	tsp. salt
¾	cup quick-cooking rolled oats
⅓	cup packed brown sugar
1	tsp. lemon zest
2	3-oz. pkg. cream cheese, softened
¼	cup butter, softened
¾	cup seedless blackberry or red or black raspberry jam
1	tsp. lemon juice

1. Preheat oven to 350°F. Grease a 9×9-inch baking pan; set aside. In a medium bowl stir together the flour, baking soda, and salt. Stir in oats, brown sugar, and lemon zest. Set aside.
2. In a large bowl beat cream cheese and butter with a mixer on medium to high 30 seconds. Add flour mixture. Beat on low until mixture is crumbly. Remove 1 cup of crumb mixture for topping; set aside.
3. Press remaining crumb mixture into prepared pan. Bake 20 minutes.
4. Meanwhile, in a small bowl stir together the jam and lemon juice. Carefully spread jam mixture over hot crust. Sprinkle with reserved 1 cup crumb mixture. Bake 15 minutes or until top is golden. Cool bars in pan on a wire rack. Cut into bars. Place bars in box. Makes 16 servings.
PER SERVING *173 cal., 7 g fat (5 g sat. fat), 20 mg chol., 121 mg sodium, 25 g carb., 0 g fiber, 2 g pro.*

CARAMEL APPLE BREAD PUDDING

PREP 15 minutes
STAND 10 minutes
BAKE 25 minutes at 350°F

4	cups dried cinnamon bread cubes* (8 to 10 slices)
⅔	cup finely chopped unpeeled tart apples (1 medium)
3	eggs, lightly beaten
2	cups whole milk
¼	cup butter, melted
½	cup sugar
1½	tsp. vanilla
1	tsp. apple pie spice
¼	tsp. salt
1	recipe Caramel Sauce

1. Preheat oven to 350°F. Grease cups of two 6-cup foil muffin pans or line with foil bake cups; set aside. In a large bowl combine the bread cubes and apples.
2. In a medium bowl combine eggs, milk, melted butter, sugar, vanilla, apple pie spice, and salt. Stir into bread mixture. Let stand 10 minutes to allow bread to soak up liquid, stirring occasionally. Evenly spoon bread mixture evenly into prepared muffin cups.
3. Place muffin pans on a baking sheet. Bake, uncovered, 25 to 30 minutes or until puffed and a knife inserted near centers comes out clean. Transfer muffin pans to a wire rack. Cool in pans on wire rack. Cover and chill up to 3 days.
4. If giving six puddings, include a jar containing half the caramel sauce. If giving 12 puddings, give a jar containing all the caramel sauce. Makes 12 servings.

*Tip For dry bread cubes, cut bread into ½-inch cubes; spread in a 15×10-inch baking pan. Bake 10 to 15 minutes at 300°F or until dry, stirring twice.
Caramel Sauce In a medium-size heavy saucepan combine ½ cup heavy cream, ½ cup butter (1 stick), ¾ cup packed brown sugar, and 2 tablespoons light-color corn syrup. Bring to boiling over medium-high heat, whisking occasionally. Reduce heat to medium. Boil gently 3 minutes. Remove from heat. Stir in 1 teaspoon vanilla. Cool sauce 15 minutes. Cover and chill any leftovers up to 2 weeks. (If chilled, let stand at room temperature 1 hour before serving).
To Reheat Caramel Sauce In a small saucepan heat caramel sauce over medium-low heat until warm, stirring occasionally.
To Reheat Bread Pudding Preheat oven to 325°F. Place foil muffin pan on a baking sheet. Bake, uncovered, 16 to 18 minutes or until heated through. Let stand 5 minutes before removing from pan.
PER SERVING *336 cal., 19 g fat (11 g sat. fat), 95 mg chol., 263 mg sodium, 39 g carb., 1 g fiber, 5 g pro.*

CARAMEL APPLE BREAD PUDDING

As a gift Cut three circles from white scrapbooking paper (a) and attach scrapbooking letter stickers (b) to the paper circles to spell "Let It Snow." Use a glue stick to attach circles to the top of a disposable foil muffin pan lid (c). Pour Caramel Sauce into a mini jam jar (d). Punch a hole in the plastic lid of muffin pan and insert and a ribbon (e).

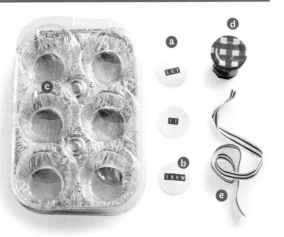

Toast to a New Year

Ring in the coming year in style and good taste.
These delicious appetizers and desserts
are worthy of celebration.

BACON-ALMOND
POTATO
CROQUETTES,
PAGE 137

EASY SALMON-AND
CHEESE-STUFFED
MUSHROOMS, PAGE 133

POMEGRANATE
CIDER SANGRIA

WARM GINGER
SIPPER

POMEGRANATE CIDER SANGRIA

PREP 25 minutes
COOL 2 hours
CHILL 4 hours

6   cups apple cider
2   cups pomegranate juice
½   cup pomegranate molasses
2   cinnamon sticks
2   whole star anise
1   orange, thinly sliced
1   apple, cored and thinly sliced
½   to 1 cup brandy (optional)

1. In a large non-aluminum pot cook and stir apple cider, pomegranate juice, and pomegranate molasses over medium heat until steaming. Add cinnamon sticks and star anise; remove from heat. Stir in orange and apple slices. Let cool. Transfer to a large pitcher.
2. Cover and refrigerate until chilled or up to 1 day. If desired, stir in brandy before serving. Makes 12 servings.
Make Ahead Sangria can be made up to 1 day ahead and served straight from the refrigerator with fruit in the pitcher.
PER SERVING *174 cal., 0 fat, 0 mg chol., 16 mg sodium, 43 g carb., 1 g fiber, 0 g pro.*

WARM GINGER SIPPER

START TO FINISH 25 minutes

4   cups water
½   cup sliced fresh ginger (2 oz.)
2   strips lemon zest
2   Tbsp. honey
     Lemon wedges

1. In a medium saucepan, bring water, ginger, and lemon zest to boiling over high. Turn off heat, cover, and steep 15 minutes. Strain mixture, discarding ginger and lemon zest. Add honey to strained mixture and serve with lemon wedges. Makes 6 servings.
PER SERVING *23 cal., 0 fat, 0 mg chol., 5 mg sodium, 6 g carb., 0 g fiber, 0 g pro.*

SWEET AND SALTY ROASTED NUTS

PREP 15 minutes
STAND 5 minutes
BAKE 35 minutes at 300°F

1   egg white
1   Tbsp. water
4   cups raw whole cashews, whole almonds, walnut halves, and/or pecan halves
3   Tbsp. packed brown sugar
1   Tbsp. ground cumin
2   tsp. chili powder
1   tsp. garlic salt
⅛   tsp. cayenne pepper

1. Preheat oven to 300°F. In a medium bowl combine egg white and the water; beat with a fork until frothy. Add nuts; toss to coat. Let stand 5 minutes.
2. Meanwhile, in a large plastic bag combine remaining ingredients. Add nuts; shake well to coat. Spread nuts in a 15×10-inch baking pan.
3. Bake 35 to 40 minutes or until nuts are toasted and coating is dry, stirring twice. Transfer to a large sheet of foil. Cool completely. Store in an airtight container at room temperature up to 5 days or freeze up to 3 months. Makes 16 servings.
PER SERVING *206 cal., 16 g fat (3 g sat. fat), 0 mg chol., 72 mg sodium, 13 g carb., 1 g fiber, 7 g pro.*

SWEET AND SALTY
ROASTED NUTS

FLATBREAD WITH
BALSAMIC
GREENS AND
PROSCIUTTO

FLATBREAD WITH BALSAMIC GREENS AND PROSCIUTTO

PREP 30 minutes
BAKE 15 minutes at 450°F

- 1 lb. purchased or Homemade Pizza Dough, at room temperature
- 1 Tbsp. finely chopped fresh rosemary
- 3 Tbsp. olive oil
- 1 large red onion, cut into ½-inch wedges (2 cups)
- ¼ tsp. freshly ground black pepper
- 6 cups kale and/or radicchio, stemmed and torn
- 3 Tbsp. balsamic vinegar
- 4 oz. Fontina or Gouda cheese, shredded
- 4 to 6 paper-thin slices prosciutto

1. Place a rack in center of oven; preheat to 450°F. Divide dough in half. On a floured surface, roll out each dough half to a 12×6-inch rectangle. Transfer both to a lightly oiled baking sheet. Sprinkle with rosemary; drizzle with 1 tablespoon olive oil. Bake 10 to 12 minutes or until golden.
2. Meanwhile, in a 12-inch skillet heat 2 tablespoons olive oil over medium heat. Add onion and black pepper. Cook 10 minutes or until tender and light brown, stirring occasionally. Add greens and vinegar; toss to coat. Cook 3 to 5 minutes or until greens are wilted and liquid has evaporated.
3. Divide cooked greens between flatbreads; top with cheese. Bake 5 minutes or until cheese is melted. Top with sliced prosciutto before serving. Makes 8 servings.
PER SERVING *575 cal., 24 g fat (7 g sat. fat), 36 mg chol., 913 mg sodium, 67 g carb., 6 g fiber, 24 g pro.*
Homemade Pizza Dough In an extra-large bowl combine 1¾ cups lukewarm water and 1½ teaspoons active dry yeast; let stand 5 minutes or until yeast is foamy. Stir in 4½ cups all-purpose flour and 2 teaspoons kosher salt. Turn dough out onto a lightly floured surface. Knead until smooth and elastic, about 3 minutes. Place in a well-greased bowl, turning to grease surface of dough. Cover with plastic; let rise at room temperature until double in size, 1½ hours. Punch dough down. Divide into quarters; shape into balls. Cover; let rest 10 minutes. This recipe makes 2 pounds; use half for this recipe.

EASY SALMON-AND-CHEESE-STUFFED MUSHROOMS

EASY SALMON-AND-CHEESE-STUFFED MUSHROOMS

PREP 15 minutes
BAKE 17 minutes at 425°F
STAND 5 minutes

- 20 large cremini or button mushrooms (about 24 oz.)
- 4 oz. thinly sliced smoked salmon (lox-style), chopped
- 1 5.2-oz. pkg. semisoft cheese with fines herbs (such as Boursin) Fresh snipped Italian parsley or chopped green onions (optional)

1. Lightly grease a 15×10-inch baking pan. Quickly rinse mushrooms; wipe caps clean with paper towels. Remove stems from mushrooms; discard or reserve for another use. Place caps, stem sides up, on prepared baking sheet.
2. Divide smoked salmon among mushroom caps, pressing down lightly. Top with about 1½ teaspoons semisoft cheese. (If desired, cover and refrigerate up to 24 hours.)
3. When ready to serve, preheat oven to 425°F. Bake mushrooms 17 to 20 minutes or until mushrooms are tender. Let stand 5 minutes before serving. If desired, sprinkle with parsley. Makes 20 servings.
PER SERVING *44 cal., 3 g fat (2 g sat. fat), 10 mg chol., 103 mg sodium, 1 g carb., 0 g fiber, 3 g pro.*
Easy Bacon-Stuffed Mushrooms Prepare as directed, except omit salmon. Cook eight slices of bacon until crisp; drain on paper towels and crumble. Stir together semisoft cheese and crumbled bacon. Spoon cheese mixture into mushrooms. Continue as directed.

CHEESE WAFERS WITH PEPPER JELLY

PREP 15 minutes
CHILL 2 hours
BAKE 8 minutes per batch at 400°F

- 2 cups all-purpose flour
- ½ cup butter, cut up
- 1 tsp. sugar
- ¼ tsp. salt
- ¼ tsp. curry powder
  Dash cayenne pepper
- 2 cups shredded sharp cheddar cheese (8 oz.)
- 4 to 5 Tbsp. water
  Jalapeño pepper jelly

1. In a food processor combine flour, butter, sugar, salt, curry powder, and cayenne pepper. Cover and pulse two or three times or until pieces are pea size. Add cheese. Cover and pulse two or three times until mixed. Add the water, 1 tablespoon at a time, pulsing after each addition just until dough is moistened.
2. Gather dough into a ball; divide dough in half. Shape each half into a 10-inch log; wrap in plastic wrap. Chill 2 to 24 hours.
3. Preheat oven to 400°F. Grease a large baking sheet or line with parchment paper. Cut logs into ¼-inch slices. Place slices 1 inch apart on prepared baking sheet. Prick slices with a fork.
4. Bake 8 to 10 minutes or just until edges start to brown. Transfer to a wire rack to cool. Serve with pepper jelly. Makes 20 servings.
PER SERVING *170 cal., 9 g fat (5 g sat. fat), 24 mg chol., 143 mg sodium, 20 g carb., 0 g fiber, 4 g pro.*

SHRIMP COCKTAIL

SHRIMP COCKTAIL

PREP 25 minutes
CHILL 2 hours

- 1½ lb. fresh or frozen large shrimp in shells
- ¾ cup chili sauce
- 2 Tbsp. lemon juice
- 2 Tbsp. thinly sliced green onion
- 1 Tbsp. prepared horseradish
- 2 tsp. Worcestershire sauce
  Several dashes bottled hot pepper sauce

1. Thaw shrimp, if frozen. Peel and devein shrimp. Cook shrimp in lightly salted boiling water 1 to 3 minutes or until shrimp turn opaque, stirring occasionally. Rinse in a colander under cold running water; drain again. Chill 2 hours or overnight.
2. For sauce, in a small bowl combine the remaining ingredients. Cover and chill until serving time. Serve shrimp with sauce. Makes 8 servings.
PER SERVING *84 cal., 0 g fat, 103 mg chol., 383 mg sodium, 8 g carb., 0 g fiber, 13 g pro.*

Herbed Shrimp Sauce Omit sauce ingredients in Step 2. In a blender combine ¼ cup each lemon juice and olive oil; 2 tablespoons each prepared horseradish and water; 2 teaspoons Dijon mustard; ½ cup each chopped fresh parsley and chopped fresh basil; 4 oil-packed dried tomatoes, drained and patted dry; and ½ teaspoon crushed red pepper. Cover and blend until nearly smooth, scraping down sides of blender as needed. Makes 8 servings.
PER SERVING *46 cal., 5 g fat (1 g sat. fat), 0 mg chol., 34 mg sodium, 1 g carb, 0 g fiber, 0 g pro.*

CHEESE WAFERS
WITH PEPPER JELLY

BACON-ALMOND
POTATO
CROQUETTES

BACON-ALMOND POTATO CROQUETTES

PREP 45 minutes
CHILL 4 hours
COOK 3 minutes per batch

4   large Yukon gold potatoes, peeled, quartered, cooked, and mashed
8   slices bacon, crisp-cooked, drained, and crumbled
⅓   cup finely chopped green onions
6   Tbsp. butter, melted
½   tsp. salt
½   tsp. ground white pepper
⅛   tsp. cayenne pepper
½   cup all-purpose flour
2   eggs
2   cups sliced almonds, chopped
    Peanut oil
    Ketchup (optional)

1. In a medium bowl combine first seven ingredients (through cayenne pepper). Cover and chill at least 4 hours.
2. Place flour in a small bowl. Place eggs in another small bowl; beat lightly with a fork. Spread almonds in a shallow dish. Shape potato mixture into 1-inch balls. Roll balls in flour, then in beaten egg; roll in almonds to coat.
3. In a heavy saucepan or deep-fat fryer heat 2 to 3 inches of oil to 375°F. Fry potato croquettes, about six at a time, in hot oil 3 to 4 minutes or until golden brown.
4. Using a slotted spoon, remove croquettes; drain on paper towels. Keep warm in a 200°F oven while frying remaining croquettes. If desired, serve croquettes with ketchup. Makes 40 servings.
Make Ahead Prepare as directed through Step 1. Cover and chill up to 24 hours. Continue as directed.
PER SERVING *73 cal., 5 g fat (2 g sat. fat), 17 mg chol., 83 mg sodium, 5 g carb., 1 g fiber, 2 g pro.*

MEATBALLS AND STUFFED ZUCCHINI

PREP 45 minutes
BAKE 50 minutes at 375°F

1   28-oz. can whole tomatoes, undrained and coarsely chopped
2   Tbsp. tomato paste
1   Tbsp. chopped fresh marjoram or oregano

MEATBALLS AND STUFFED ZUCCHINI

1   Tbsp. extra-virgin olive oil
1½ tsp. fine sea salt
6   medium zucchini (about 3 lb.), ends trimmed
1   lb. 90% lean ground beef
2   cups lightly packed fresh bread crumbs*
2   eggs, lightly beaten
½   cup finely shredded Parmesan or Pecorino Romano cheese (1 oz.)
¼   cup chopped fresh Italian parsley
2   Tbsp. half-and-half or milk
3   cloves garlic, minced
¼   tsp. freshly ground black pepper

1. For tomato sauce, in a medium bowl combine the first four ingredients (through oil) and ½ tsp. of the salt; set aside.
2. Using a corer, hollow out each zucchini, being careful not to pierce the sides. Discard center flesh; set zucchini aside.
3. Preheat oven to 375°F. In a large bowl combine beef, bread crumbs, eggs, cheese, parsley, half-and-half, garlic, remaining 1 teaspoon salt, and black

pepper. Divide mixture in half. Spoon half the meat mixture into zucchini, packing lightly (filling will expand during baking). Shape remaining meat mixture into twelve 1½-inch meatballs.
4. Spoon ½ cup of the tomato sauce into a 3-quart rectangular baking dish. Arrange zucchini in dish; spoon half of remaining sauce on top; cover with foil. Arrange meatballs in a 2-quart baking dish; spoon remaining sauce over meatballs.
5. Bake zucchini 50 minutes or until thermometer inserted in meat mixture registers 160°F and zucchini is tender, turning zucchini once. Bake meatballs, uncovered, the last 30 minutes or until done (160°F). Cool zucchini slightly; slice into 1-inch rounds. Makes 6 servings.
*Tip For fresh bread crumbs, trim crust off day-old bread. Tear or cut into pieces. Pulse in a food processor, until crumbs form.
PER SERVING *354 cal., 16 g fat (6 g sat. fat), 120 mg chol., 1,142 mg sodium, 26 g carb., 6 g fiber, 27 g pro.*

MUHAMMARA

MUHAMMARA

START TO FINISH 10 minutes

½   cup fine dry bread crumbs
½   cup walnuts, toasted
⅓   cup chopped red onion
1   large garlic clove, halved
1   tsp. ground cumin
½   tsp. crushed red pepper
1   16-oz. jar roasted red sweet
     peppers, drained
1   cup cottage cheese
1   Tbsp. pomegranate molasses
1   tsp. lemon juice
     Chopped fresh Italian parsley
     Olive oil (optional)
     Pita bread, naan, and/or pita chips

1. In a food processor or high-power blender combine first six ingredients (through crushed red pepper). Cover and pulse until finely chopped. Add roasted peppers; cover and pulse until combined. Add cottage cheese, pomegranate molasses, and lemon juice. Cover and pulse until dip reaches desired consistency.
2. Transfer dip to a serving bowl. Sprinkle with parsley and, if desired, drizzle with olive oil and/or additional pomegranate molasses. Serve with pita bread, naan, and/or pita chips. Makes 12 servings.
PER SERVING *90 cal., 5 g fat (1 g sat. fat), 3 mg chol., 102 mg sodium, 9 g carb., 1 g fiber, 3 g pro.*

DRIED BEEF-CREAM CHEESE BOMBS

PREP 20 minutes
BAKE 12 minutes at 375°F

     Nonstick cooking spray
2   2.5-oz. pkg. dried beef or 5 oz.
     deli-style thinly sliced cooked ham,
     finely chopped
1   8-oz. pkg. cream cheese, softened
1   Tbsp. horseradish mustard or
     other deli-style mustard
2   8-oz. cans refrigerated dough
     sheets (such as Pillsbury Recipe
     Creations seamless dough sheets)
2   large dill pickle spears, each cut
     into 6 chunks (12 chunks total)

1. Preheat oven to 375°F. Coat twelve 2½-inch muffin cups with cooking spray.
2. For filling, in a bowl stir together dried beef, cream cheese, and mustard. Set aside.
3. Unroll one dough sheet onto a lightly floured work surface and pat into a 12×8-inch rectangle. With a pizza cutter, cut dough evenly into six 4-inch squares. Place 2 tablespoons of the cream cheese mixture in a mound on the center of each round. Press a pickle chunk into each cream cheese mound. Repeat with remaining dough sheet and filling.
4. For each cheese bomb, pull dough up to cover filling completely; pinch seams firmly to seal. Place bombs, seam sides up, in prepared muffin cups. Bake 12 to 15 minutes or until golden brown. Serve hot. Makes 12 servings.
Make Ahead Let cheese bombs cool completely. Place in 1-gallon resealable freezer bags and freeze up to 1 month. To reheat, wrap each cheese bomb in foil and bake 15 to 20 minutes at 350°F or until heated through.
PER SERVING *204 cal., 12 g fat (6 g sat. fat), 30 mg chol., 763 mg sodium, 17 g carb., 0 g fiber, 7 g pro.*

DRIED BEEF–CREAM
CHEESE BOMBS

BASIL TOMATO TART

PREP 30 minutes
BAKE 12 minutes at 450°F plus
35 minutes at 375°F

½   14.1-oz. pkg. rolled refrigerated
     unbaked piecrust (1 crust)
1½ cups shredded mozzarella cheese
     (6 oz.)
5   roma tomatoes or 4 medium
     tomatoes
1   cup loosely packed fresh basil
     leaves
2   cloves garlic, halved
½   cup mayonnaise
¼   cup grated Parmesan cheese
⅛   tsp. white pepper

1. Preheat oven to 450°F. Let piecrust
stand according to package directions.
Unroll piecrust into a 9-inch quiche
dish or pie plate. Fold under extra
pastry even with edge of dish; crimp
edge as desired. Do not prick pastry.
Line pastry with a double-thickness of
foil. Bake 8 minutes. Remove foil. Bake
4 to 5 minutes more or until set and
dry. Remove from oven. Reduce oven
temperature to 375°F. Sprinkle partially
baked pastry shell with ½ cup of the
mozzarella cheese. Cool slightly on a
wire rack.
2. Cut tomatoes into wedges; drain on
paper towels. Arrange tomato wedges
on cheese in pastry shell. In a food
processor combine basil and garlic;
cover and pulse until coarsely chopped.
Sprinkle on tomatoes.
3. In a medium bowl combine remaining
1 cup mozzarella cheese, mayonnaise,
Parmesan cheese, and pepper. Spread
cheese mixture on tomato mixture,
covering top completely.
4. Bake 35 to 40 minutes or until top
is golden and bubbly. Serve warm.
If desired, top with additional basil
and Parmesan cheese. Makes 8 to
12 appetizer servings.
Make Ahead Prepare and bake pastry
shell; cut tomatoes into wedges and
drain. Cover pastry and tomatoes and
let stand at room temperature up to
2 hours. Prepare cheese mixture; cover
and chill up to 2 hours. Assemble and
bake tart as directed.
PER SERVING *275 cal., 21 g fat
(6 g sat. fat), 24 mg chol., 369 mg
sodium, 17 g carb., 1 g fiber, 8 g pro.*

LEMONGRASS
CHICKEN WONTONS

PREP 45 minutes
COOK 3 minutes per batch

1   egg, lightly beaten
2   green onions, finely chopped
1   Tbsp. soy sauce
2   tsp. mirin
1   tsp. toasted sesame oil
2   Tbsp. minced lemongrass
1   Tbsp. minced fresh ginger
1   tsp. salt
1   clove garlic, peeled and minced
1   lb. uncooked ground chicken
32 wonton wrappers

1. For filling, in a large bowl whisk
together the egg, green onions, soy
sauce, mirin, and sesame oil. In a
spice grinder or small food processor
combine lemongrass, ginger, salt, and
garlic. Cover and process to a smooth
paste. Add to egg mixture. Add ground
chicken; use hands to gently combine.
2. Line a baking sheet with parchment
paper and prepare a small dish of cool
water. In the center of each wonton
wrapper, place 2 teaspoons of filling in
the center of the wrapper. Brush edges
of wonton wrapper with water. Fold
wrapper over to seal in a triangle shape,
gently pressing wrapper to push out air.
(If you like, fold two corners together
and bring them together opposite side
the filling to make a hat shape.) Place
filled wontons on prepared baking sheet.
Refrigerate or freeze until ready to cook.
3. To cook wontons, bring a pot of
salted water to boiling. Cook in batches
of six for 3 to 4 minutes or until wontons
float. Makes 16 servings.
PER SERVING *85 cal., 3 g fat (1 g sat. fat),
37 mg chol., 270 mg sodium, 8 g carb.,
0 g fiber, 6 g pro.*

BABA GANOUSH

PREP 25 minutes
ROAST 30 minutes at 425°F

3   medium eggplants
     (about 1 lb. each)
½   cup tahini (sesame seed paste)
¼   cup fresh Italian parsley leaves
¼   cup lemon juice
2   cloves garlic, peeled
1   tsp. kosher salt
1   Tbsp. olive oil
     Crushed red pepper (optional)
     Toasted baguette slices

1. Preheat oven to 425°F. Line a 15×10-
inch baking pan with foil. Prick eggplants
all over with a fork. Place in prepared
pan. Bake 30 to 40 minutes or until very
soft and skin is charred. Cool until easy
to handle.
2. Remove and discard skins from
eggplant. Place eggplant in a food
processor or blender. Add the next five
ingredients (through salt). Cover and
pulse until nearly smooth, leaving some
pieces of eggplant. Season to taste with
additional salt. Transfer baba ganoush
to a serving bowl. Drizzle with olive oil
and, if desired, sprinkle with crushed
red pepper. Serve with baguette slices.
Makes 18 servings.
Make Ahead Transfer baba ganoush
to an airtight storage container. Cover
and chill up to 3 days. Let stand at room
temperature before serving.
PER SERVING *67 cal., 4 g fat (1 g sat. fat),
0 mg chol., 114 mg sodium, 6 g carb.,
3 g fiber, 2 g pro.*

APPLE,
CRANBERRY,
AND PECAN
GALETTE

In a small bowl combine ⅔ cup sugar, the cinnamon, and allspice. Sprinkle apples with sugar mixture; stir to coat. Stir in cranberries.

3. To assemble, if necessary, let dough stand at room temperature 30 minutes or until soft enough to roll out. On a well-floured surface, roll dough into an oval about ⅛ inch thick (about 18×12 inches). Transfer to a baking sheet lined with foil. Spread pecans on pastry, leaving a 2-inch border. Spoon fruit on pecans. Use foil to bring pastry edge over fruit, crimping and folding as needed. In a small bowl blend egg and water. Brush pastry with egg wash. Sprinkle lightly with additional sugar.

4. Bake 15 minutes. Reduce heat to 350°F and bake 30 to 40 minutes more or until apples are tender and crust is deep golden brown. For easier slicing, let cool before serving. Makes 10 servings.

*Tip To toast a large amount of nuts, preheat oven to 350°F. Spread nuts on a shallow baking pan. Bake 5 to 10 minutes or until fragrant and lightly browned. Cool before chopping.

**Tip To make pastry in a food processor, combine ingredients in Step 1, pulsing a few times at each stage. Add water slowly, while pulsing, until dough begins to come together yet still looks crumbly.

PER SERVING *418 cal., 25 g fat (8 g sat. fat), 43 mg chol., 185 mg sodium, 48 g carb., 4 g fiber, 5 g pro.*

APPLE, CRANBERRY, AND PECAN GALETTE

PREP 35 minutes
CHILL 1 hour
BAKE 15 minutes at 425°F plus 30 minutes at 350°F

2   cups all-purpose flour
⅔   cup plus 2 to 3 Tbsp. raw or
     granulated sugar
¾   tsp. salt
½   cup cold unsalted butter, cut up
⅓   cup shortening
¼   to ½ cup ice water
4   medium cooking apples; peeled,
     cored, and sliced ¼ inch thick
2   Tbsp. fresh squeezed orange juice
1   tsp. ground cinnamon
½   tsp. ground allspice
1   cup fresh cranberries, coarsely
     chopped

1   cup chopped pecans, toasted*
1   egg
1   Tbsp. water

1. For pastry, in a large bowl** combine flour, 1 tablespoon sugar, and salt. Using a pastry blender, cut butter and shortening into flour mixture until it resembles coarse crumbs. Sprinkle 1 tablespoon of ice water over part of mixture. Toss with a fork to moisten. Continue adding water 1 tablespoon at a time, moving moistened dough to the side of bowl, until mixture is moistened and comes together when squeezed. Form dough into a disc and wrap with plastic wrap. Refrigerate at least 1 hour or up to 24 hours.

2. Preheat oven to 425°F. For filling, place apples in a large bowl and sprinkle with orange juice; toss to coat.

S'MORES CHEESECAKE

PREP 45 minutes
BAKE 40 minutes at 375°F
COOL 45 minutes
BROIL 30 seconds
CHILL 4 hours

1½   cups finely crushed graham
     crackers
1   Tbsp. sugar
⅓   cup butter, melted
4   oz. semisweet chocolate, chopped
3   8-oz. pkg. cream cheese, softened
¾   cup sugar
½   cup sour cream
2   tsp. vanilla
2   Tbsp. all-purpose flour
3   eggs
1   recipe Ganache
3   cups tiny marshmallows
     Broken graham crackers (optional)
     Chopped semisweet chocolate
     (optional)

1. Preheat oven to 375°F. For crust, stir together crushed graham crackers and 1 tablespoon sugar. Drizzle with melted butter; toss to coat. Press crumb mixture onto bottom and about 1½ inches up sides of a 9-inch springform pan with removable bottom.

2. For filling, in a small heavy saucepan stir the 4 ounces of chocolate over low heat until melted; cool slightly. In a medium bowl beat cream cheese, ¾ cup sugar, the sour cream, and vanilla with a mixer on medium until smooth. Add flour; beat well. Add cooled chocolate. Add eggs; beat on low just until combined.

3. Pour filling into crust-lined pan. Place pan in a shallow baking pan. Bake 40 to 45 minutes or until center appears nearly set when gently shaken (center may look soft but will set up as it cools).

4. Cool cheesecake in pan on a wire rack 15 minutes. Using a small metal spatula, loosen crust from sides of pan. Cool 30 minutes. Remove sides of pan (leave cheesecake in shallow baking pan).

5. Preheat broiler. Spoon Ganache over top of cheesecake, spreading evenly and allowing it to drip down sides (set any remaining ganache aside). Pile marshmallows in center of cheesecake.

6. Broil 4 to 5 inches from the heat 30 to 60 seconds or just until marshmallows are golden (watch closely to prevent burning). Cover loosely; chill at least 4 hours. Before serving, drizzle with any remaining ganache. If desired, top with broken graham crackers and additional chopped chocolate. Makes 12 servings.

Ganache In a medium saucepan bring 1 cup heavy cream just to boiling over medium-high heat. Remove saucepan from heat. Add 12 ounces chopped milk chocolate, semisweet chocolate, or bittersweet chocolate (do not stir). Let stand 5 minutes. Stir until smooth. Cool 15 minutes. Makes 2 cups.

PER SERVING *583 cal., 39 g fat (22 g sat. fat), 147 mg chol., 366 mg sodium, 53 g carb., 2 g fiber, 8 g pro.*

S'MORES
CHEESECAKE

CANDY-CRUNCH PEANUT
BUTTER BARS,
PAGE 154

TUSCAN TORTELLINI
SOUP, PAGE 148

Guest-Friendly Fare

Prepare to host out-of-town family and friends with delicious recipes
perfect for casual, relaxed company meals.

CINNAMON NUTS

CINNAMON NUTS

PREP 20 minutes
BAKE 40 minutes at 300°F

1 egg white
1 Tbsp. water
1 tsp. vanilla
1½ lb. walnut halves and/or pecan
   halves
1 cup sugar
2 Tbsp. ground cinnamon
1 tsp. freshly grated nutmeg or
   ½ tsp. ground nutmeg

1. Preheat oven to 300°F. Grease a
15×10-inch baking pan. In an extra-large
bowl beat together egg white, the water,
and vanilla with a fork. Add nuts, tossing
to coat.
2. In a small bowl combine sugar,
cinnamon, and nutmeg. Sprinkle sugar
mixture over nut mixture, tossing to coat.
Spread nuts in prepared baking pan.
3. Bake 40 minutes or until nuts are
toasted and crisp, stirring once halfway
through baking time. Spread nuts on
waxed paper; cool. If necessary, break
into pieces. Makes 24 servings.
To Store Place nuts in an airtight
container; cover. Store at room
temperature up to 2 weeks.
PER SERVING *221 cal., 19 g fat (2 g sat.
fat), 0 mg chol., 3 mg sodium, 13 g carb.,
2 g fiber, 4 g pro.*

BACON AND TOMATO POTATO SKINS

PREP 45 minutes
BAKE 10 minutes at 450°F

6 large baking potatoes
2 tsp. vegetable oil
1 tsp. chili powder
2 dashes hot sauce
⅔ cup chopped crisp-cooked bacon
1 medium tomato, finely chopped
2 Tbsp. finely chopped green onion
1 cup shredded cheddar cheese (4 oz.)
½ cup sour cream (optional)

1. Scrub potatoes thoroughly and
prick with a fork. Arrange on a plate.
Microwave, uncovered, 17 to 22 minutes
or until almost tender, rearranging once.
(Or bake potatoes 40 to 45 minutes at
425°F or until tender.) Cool. Preheat
oven to 450°F.
2. Halve each potato lengthwise. Scoop
out the flesh of each potato half, leaving
about a ¼-inch shell. Cover and chill
leftover potato flesh for another use.
Combine the cooking oil, chili powder,
and hot pepper sauce. Brush insides of
potato skins with oil mixture. Cut skins in
half lengthwise. Return to baking sheet.
Sprinkle skins with bacon, tomato, and
green onion. Top with cheese.
3. Bake 10 to 12 minutes or until cheese
is melted and skins are heated through.
If desired, serve with sour cream. Makes
24 servings.
PER SERVING *84 cal., 3 g fat (1 g sat. fat),
8 mg chol., 97 mg sodium, 11 g carb.,
1 g fiber, 4 g pro.*

BACON AND TOMATO
POTATO SKINS

BUTTERNUT-FETA GALETTE

PREP 30 minutes
ROAST 25 minutes at 425°F
BAKE 35 minutes at 375°F

2 lb. butternut squash, peeled, seeded, and cut into ½-inch cubes
2 Tbsp. olive oil
1 Tbsp. chopped fresh thyme
½ tsp. salt
¼ tsp. black pepper
1 recipe Pastry for Single Crust Pie (page 90)
½ cup crumbled feta cheese
   Milk (optional)
   Fresh thyme
   Honey

1. Preheat oven to 425°F. Place squash in a shallow baking pan. Drizzle with oil; sprinkle with thyme, salt, and black pepper; toss to coat. Roast, uncovered, 25 minutes or until tender, stirring once. Reduce oven temperature to 375°F.

2. Meanwhile, prepare pastry. On a large sheet of lightly floured parchment paper, roll pastry to a 13-inch circle. Slide parchment and pastry onto a baking sheet.

3. Mound squash in center of pastry, leaving 1½-inch border. Using parchment, lift and fold pastry edge over filling, pleating as necessary and leaving center vegetables exposed. Sprinkle filling with feta. If desired, brush pastry with milk.

4. Bake 35 to 40 minutes or until crust is golden. Cool slightly before serving. Sprinkle with additional thyme and drizzle with honey. Makes 10 servings.
PER SERVING *246 cal., 14 g fat (6 g sat. fat), 19 mg chol., 343 mg sodium, 27 g carb., 2 g fiber, 4 g pro.*

TUSCAN TORTELLINI SOUP

PREP 20 minutes
SLOW COOK 6 hours (low) or 3 hours (high) plus 30 minutes (high)

3 14.5-oz. cans reduced-sodium chicken broth
1 28-oz. can diced tomatoes with basil, garlic, and oregano; undrained
1 fennel bulb, trimmed, quartered, cored, and sliced
1 cup chopped onion
8 cups chopped kale
1 9-oz. pkg. refrigerated cheese-filled tortellini or ravioli
2 Tbsp. chopped fresh oregano
1 to 2 Tbsp. heavy cream
½ cup grated Parmesan cheese

1. In a 6-quart slow cooker combine broth, tomatoes, fennel, and onion. Cover and cook on low 6 hours or high 3 hours.

2. If using low, turn to high. Stir in kale, tortellini, and oregano. Cover; cook 30 minutes more or until tortellini are tender. Stir in cream. Sprinkle servings with cheese. Makes 6 servings.
PER SERVING *294 cal., 7 g fat (3 g sat. fat), 25 mg chol., 1,222 mg sodium, 46 g carb., 7 g fiber, 16 g pro.*

BUTTERNUT-FETA GALETTE

TUSCAN
TORTELLINI SOUP

MINI ITALIAN
WHITE BEAN AND
KALE POT PIES

MINI ITALIAN WHITE BEAN AND KALE POT PIES

PREP 30 minutes
COOK 15 minutes
BAKE 30 minutes at 400°F
STAND 15 minutes

2	Tbsp. butter
1	fennel bulb, quartered, cored, and thinly sliced
1	cup chopped onion
3	cloves garlic, minced
1	tsp. fresh snipped oregano
½	tsp. salt
¼	tsp. crushed red pepper
1	medium bunch kale, stemmed and chopped (8 cups)
⅓	cup all-purpose flour
1	14.5-oz. can vegetable broth
¼	cup plus 1 Tbsp. heavy cream, half-and-half, or whole milk
1	15-oz. can cannellini beans, rinsed and drained
⅓	cup oil-packed dried tomatoes, drained and chopped
1	recipe Pastry for Single-Crust Pie (page 90)
2	Tbsp. Parmesan cheese

1. Preheat oven to 400°F. Arrange six 10- to 12-ounce ramekins in a shallow baking pan lined with foil. For filling, in a Dutch oven melt butter over medium heat. Add fennel and onion; cook and stir 5 minutes or until tender. Add garlic, oregano, salt, and crushed red pepper. Cook and stir 30 seconds. Add kale; cook until wilted, 3 to 5 minutes more. Add flour; cook and stir 1 minute. Stir in broth and ¼ cup cream, scraping up any browned bits. Cook and stir until thickened and bubbly. Stir in beans and tomatoes. Divide filling among ramekins.
2. Prepare Pastry for Single-Crust Pie, adding 2 tablespoons Parmesan cheese to flour and salt mixture. Divide pastry into six portions. Roll each pastry between sheets of parchment paper from center to edges into a circle ½ inch larger than ramekins. Top filling with pastry. Fold pastry under even with edges; press to seal. Cut a few slits in pastry. Brush top with 1 tablespoon cream.
3. Bake 30 to 35 minutes or until pastry is golden and centers are bubbly. Let stand 15 minutes before serving. Makes 6 servings.
PER SERVING *502 cal., 27 g fat (13 g sat. fat), 46 mg chol., 954 mg sodium, 55 g carb., 9 g fiber, 13 g pro.*

QUESADILLAS

QUESADILLAS

PREP 25 minutes
COOK 8 minutes per batch

1	Tbsp. vegetable oil
8	oz. thinly sliced boneless beef sirloin steak; skinless, boneless chicken breast; or peeled and deveined shrimp; or 1 cup canned black or pinto beans
2	cups corn kernels and/or thinly sliced mushrooms, onion, zucchini, and/or sweet peppers
1	to 2 medium jalapeños, seeded if desired, and sliced or coarsely chopped (optional) (tip, page 30)
4	6-inch white corn or flour tortillas Nonstick cooking spray
2	cups shredded cheddar cheese, Chihuahua, and/or Colby and Monterey Jack (4 oz.)
2	Tbsp. chopped fresh cilantro Toppings, such as guacamole, pico de gallo, sour cream, and/or chopped tomato (optional)

1. For filling, in an extra-large skillet heat oil over medium-high heat. Add meat, chicken, or shrimp. Cook and stir 3 to 5 minutes. Stir in vegetables and, if using, jalapeño. Cook 3 to 5 minutes or just until vegetables are tender, stirring occasionally. Remove from heat. If using beans, stir them into vegetables.
2. Heat a large skillet over medium heat. Lightly coat one side of each tortilla with cooking spray. Sprinkle half of each tortilla, coated side down, with ¼ cup cheese. Top with one-fourth of the filling; sprinkle with cilantro and ¼ cup cheese.
3. Fold tortilla in half, pressing gently to seal. Cook quesadillas 8 to 10 minutes or until cheese is melted and tortillas are light brown, turning once. Cut quesadillas into wedges; serve warm. If desired, serve with toppings. Makes 8 servings.
PER SERVING *117 cal., 7 g fat (2 g sat. fat), 12 mg chol., 82 mg sodium, 10 g carb., 2 g fiber, 4 g pro.*

BUTTERNUT SQUASH
AND SAUSAGE
ENCHILADAS

BUTTERNUT SQUASH AND SAUSAGE ENCHILADAS

PREP 30 minutes
BAKE 25 minutes at 350°F

1	recipe Easy Enchilada Sauce
12	oz. peeled, seeded butternut squash cut into ½-inch cubes (2½ cups)*
12	oz. uncooked bulk Italian sausage
1	clove garlic, minced
12	6-inch corn tortillas, warmed
1½	cups shredded Monterey Jack cheese or sharp cheddar cheese (6 oz.)
	Chopped fresh cilantro and/or sour cream (optional)

1. Preheat oven to 350°F. Lightly grease a 3-quart rectangular baking dish. Prepare Easy Enchilada Sauce. Place a steamer basket in a large saucepan; add water to just below bottom of basket. Bring water to boiling. Add squash to basket. Cover and steam 5 minutes. Remove from heat.
2. Meanwhile, in a large skillet cook sausage and garlic over medium heat until browned; drain off any fat. Stir in steamed squash.
3. Spread about 1 cup sauce in prepared dish. Fill each tortilla with 1 tablespoon cheese, about ¼ cup squash mixture, and 1 tablespoon sauce. Bring sides around filling to enclose and place, seam sides down, in dish. Spoon any remaining filling around tortillas in dish. Pour remaining sauce over enchiladas.
4. Bake, covered, 20 minutes. Sprinkle with remaining cheese. Bake 5 minutes more. If desired, sprinkle with cilantro and serve with Mexican crema. Makes 6 servings.
*Tip To save time, use precut butternut squash. Cut large pieces into ½-inch cubes.
Easy Enchilada Sauce In a medium saucepan heat 2 tablespoons vegetable oil over medium heat. Stir in 2 tablespoons all-purpose flour; cook and stir 2 minutes. Add 2 tablespoons chili powder, 1 teaspoon ground cumin, and ½ teaspoon garlic powder. Cook and stir 30 seconds. Add one 15-ounce can tomato sauce and one 14.5-ounce can reduced-sodium chicken broth; whisk until smooth. Cook and stir over medium-high heat until boiling. Reduce

ROASTED
BROCCOLI
STEAKS

PAN-ROASTED
PEPPERS

heat and simmer 1 minute. Remove from heat. Season to taste with hot sauce.

PER SERVING *510 cal., 33 g fat (12 g sat. fat), 68 mg chol., 1,167 mg sodium, 35 g carb., 6 g fiber, 20 g pro.*

ROASTED BROCCOLI STEAKS

START TO FINISH 35 minutes

2   oranges
3   Tbsp. olive oil
2   cloves garlic, minced
¾   tsp. kosher salt
3   heads broccoli (1½ to 1¾ lb.)
       Cooked orzo pasta (optional)
⅓   cup pine nuts, toasted
       (tip, page 34)
¼   cup freshly grated Parmesan
       cheese
       Small fresh basil leaves
       Freshly ground black pepper

1. Preheat oven to 450°F. Line a baking sheet with foil. Remove 1 teaspoon zest and squeeze ⅓ cup juice from one orange; cut remaining orange into wedges.
2. For dressing, in a screw-top jar combine orange zest and juice, 2 tablespoons oil, the garlic, and ¼ teaspoon salt. Cover and shake well.
3. Trim broccoli stems to 3 inches long. Cut broccoli heads lengthwise into ¾-inch "steaks." Brush broccoli with remaining 1 tablespoon oil and sprinkle with remaining ½ teaspoon salt. Arrange on prepared baking sheet. Roast 20 to 25 minutes or until tender and lightly browned, turning once. Drizzle with dressing.
4. If desired, serve broccoli steaks over orzo. Top with pine nuts, cheese, basil, and pepper. Serve with orange wedges. Makes 4 servings.

PER SERVING *274 cal., 20 g fat (3 g sat. fat), 4 mg chol., 357 mg sodium, 20 g carb., 6 g fiber, 8 g sugars, 8 g pro.*

PAN-ROASTED PEPPERS

START TO FINISH 20 minutes

3   red, yellow, and/or green sweet
       peppers, seeded and cut into
       1-inch-wide strips
1   medium onion, cut into thin
       wedges
2   cloves garlic, thinly sliced
1   Tbsp. olive oil
1   Tbsp. snipped fresh herbs (such as
       basil, thyme and/or oregano)
1   Tbsp. balsamic vinegar
       Salt and black pepper

1. In an extra-large skillet cook peppers, onion, and garlic in olive oil over medium-high about 5 minutes or just until tender. Add fresh herbs and balsamic vinegar. Season to taste with salt and pepper; toss to coat. Makes 6 servings.

PER SERVING *64 cal., 2 g fat (0 g sat. fat), 0 mg chol., 54 mg sodium, 9 g carb., 2 g fiber, 1 g pro.*

COFFEE NUT TORTE

plastic wrap. Cool to room temperature (do not stir). In a large bowl beat ¾ cup softened butter 30 seconds. Add 2 cups powdered sugar, 2 tablespoons cocoa powder, and 1 teaspoon vanilla. Beat on medium until light and fluffy. Add cooled milk mixture to butter mixture, half at a time, beating on low after each addition until smooth. Beat in 4 to 6 cups powdered sugar until spreading consistency.

PER SERVING *655 cal., 21 g fat (9 g sat. fat), 137 mg chol., 183 mg sodium, 113 g carb., 1 g fiber, 7 g pro.*

CANDY-CRUNCH PEANUT BUTTER BARS

PREP 30 minutes
CHILL 1 hour

30	peanut butter sandwich cookies with peanut butter filling
¼	tsp. salt
½	cup butter, melted
2	cups powdered sugar
1⅓	cups creamy peanut butter
½	cup butter, softened
2	Tbsp. heavy cream
½	cup finely crushed burnt peanuts or other candy-coated peanuts
1	cup semisweet chocolate pieces
½	cup creamy peanut butter
	Coarsely crushed burnt peanuts or other candy-coated peanuts

1. Line a 13×9-inch pan with foil, extending foil over edges of pan; set aside. For crust, in a food processor combine peanut butter cookies and salt. Cover and process until fine crumbs form. Add melted butter. Cover and process with several on/off pulses just until combined. Press mixture evenly into prepared pan.
2. For filling, in a large bowl beat powdered sugar, 1⅓ cups peanut butter, softened butter, and cream on low to medium until smooth. Stir in ½ cup peanuts. Carefully spread filling on crust.
3. In a small heavy saucepan stir chocolate and ½ cup peanut butter over low heat until melted. Spread over layers in pan. Sprinkle with additional peanuts.
4. Cover and chill 1 hour or until set. Using edges of foil, lift uncut bars out of pan. Cut into bars. Makes 48 servings.
PER SERVING *182 cal., 12 g fat (5 g sat. fat), 11 mg chol., 127 mg sodium, 17 g carb., 1 g fiber, 4 g pro.*

COFFEE NUT TORTE

PREP 30 minutes
BAKE 20 minutes at 350°F
COOL 10 minutes

6	eggs
2	cups all-purpose flour
1	Tbsp. baking powder
1½	cups sugar
½	cup strong brewed coffee or espresso, room temperature
1	cup ground walnuts or pecans
1	recipe Creamy Butter Frosting Chopped walnuts or pecans (optional)

1. Separate eggs. Allow egg yolks and egg whites to stand at room temperature 30 minutes. Grease the bottoms of three 9×1½-inch round cake pans. Line pans with waxed paper; grease waxed paper. Set pans aside. In a medium bowl stir together flour and baking powder.
2. Preheat oven to 350°F. In a large bowl beat egg yolks, sugar, and coffee with a mixer on low until combined.

Beat on high 5 minutes or until satin smooth. Add flour mixture and beat until combined; stir in nuts. Set aside.
3. Thoroughly wash beaters. In an extra-large bowl beat egg whites on medium until stiff peaks form (tips stand straight). Gradually fold batter into beaten egg whites until combined. Pour into prepared baking pans.
4. Bake 20 to 25 minutes or until cake tops spring back when lightly touched (centers may dip slightly). Cool cake layers on wire racks 10 minutes. Remove cake layers from pans; remove waxed paper. Cool completely on wire racks. Spread ½ cup Creamy Butter Frosting on each layer; stack layers. Frost sides of cake with remaining frosting. If you like, garnish with chopped nuts. Loosely cover and chill cake up to 3 days. Makes 12 servings.

Creamy Butter Frosting In a small saucepan whisk ½ cup milk into 2 teaspoons cornstarch. Cook and stir over medium heat until thickened and slightly bubbly. Reduce heat; cook and stir 2 minutes more. Stir in 1 tablespoon rum, if desired. Cover surface with

CANDY-CRUNCH
PEANUT BUTTER BARS

Index